The
Syncretic
Society

The
Syncretic
Society

Felipe García Casals

TRANSLATED FROM THE FRENCH BY GUY DANIELS
WITH A FOREWORD BY ALFRED G. MEYER

M. E. Sharpe, Inc.
WHITE PLAINS, N.Y.

English text © 1980 by M. E. Sharpe, Inc.
901 North Broadway, White Plains, N.Y. 10603

Library of Congress Cataloging in Publication Data

Casals, Felipe Garcia.
    The syncretic society.

    "Published simultaneously as vol. X, no. 4 of *International Journal of Politics.*"
    1. Socialism in Eastern Europe. 2. Europe, Eastern—Social conditions. 3. Europe, Eastern—Economic conditions. 4. Social classes—Europe, Eastern. I. Title.
HX237.C37   335′.00947   80-6455
ISBN 0-87332-176-6

Printed in the United States of America

CONTENTS

FOREWORD

Felipe García Casals is one of the pseudonyms adopted by an East European official occupying a high managerial position. He or she is a veteran member of the country's ruling communist party and has enjoyed close personal relations with the country's current leader.

Through her or his high position in the country's cultural bureaucracy—by this I mean the administration of art, science, education, mass communications and/or entertainment—and by virtue of the professional training and experience which led to this position, Casals has had recurrent opportunities for contact and friendship with colleagues in Western Europe and the United States. In 1977, one such friend received the manuscript entitled "Theses," with indications that Casals wished to have it published and discussed in the English-speaking world. The friend, in turn, asked me to help him in this. My first step was to ask a graduate student of mine to help me translate the manuscript from its French original—a difficult task because the style of the document was highly condensed, its language opaque; and its author could not be consulted about the resulting obscurities.

Translated into English, the article was read and discussed at a panel I organized for this purpose at the 1978 annual meeting of the American Political Science Association.

Since then, through the same pipeline, of which I know only the last link, a second manuscript, called "Introduction," has come into my possession. Written in different form, it obviously is a continuation of the Theses. Both articles seek to analyze Soviet society and, by implication, its client societies in Eastern Europe; but the Theses dwell more on the genesis of Stalin, while the Introduction has a bit more to say about its trends of development or self-perpetuation. These are subtle differences in emphasis. In effect, the two pieces deal with one and the same subject and can be read in either of the two possible sequences. They differ in style and emphasis and complement each other.

Together, these two essays constitute one of the most interesting and provocative pieces of "underground" literature to emerge from the socialist world. I shall allow myself a few comments on the method, the findings, the style, and the significance of this document.

Casals has made an attempt to apply Marxist categories and concepts rigorously to a critique of the Soviet system and its dependent systems of Eastern Europe. Steeped in the ideological classics of Marxism and Leninism, the author assumes a similar familiarity with this holy writ on the part of the reader. One will have to have read *Das Kapital* and the classics of Leninism, one will have to be acquainted with the history of the Russian revolution and the Soviet state in order to understand many of the statements made by Casals, especially in those passages that deal with economics.

Casals appears to be familiar also with a good deal of Western literature on the Soviet Union and with Western social science in general, though we cannot, from these essays, assess the precise range of this familiarity. There are occasional references to structuralism; and the entire analysis, with its stress on the total system and the universal relatedness of all its discrete parts, reminds us of Parsonian systems theory, of structural-function-alism.

There is, however, a crucial difference between the theory of Casals and that of Parsons and his students. In the Parsonian model, all structures tend to be eufunctional, as system-mainte-nance devices. Everything fits; the system is a going concern. Dysfunctionalities tend to be sloughed off somehow. But Casals describes a system in which the major constituent elements do not fit each other. Stalinism, according to Casals, is a nonsystem or unsystem, an incoherent structure of dysfunctional parts, hence a monstrosity. The author of these essays is careful to dis-tinguish such systemic incoherence (he or she calls it "syncre-tism") from the Marxist category of contradiction; and it is here that the basic assumptions, method, and thrust of this work dif-fer from both Marxism and Parsonian systems theory. Both these latter are infused with a positive, optimistic spirit. In struc-tural-functional theory, the emphasis being placed on eufunc-tionality, the tendency most often is apologetic; deviant phe-nomena are simply dismissed, their origins often left unexplained. Marxism, to be sure, focuses on failures and contradictions; it is as critical as structural-functionalism is apologetic. But, as Casals is careful to point out, the Marxist category of contradiction carries in itself the idea of dialectical transcendence. Hence, contradictions point to their own resolution; they contain the promise of progress. Not so the notion of the syncretic society. Its dysfunctionalities can do no more than reproduce themselves perpetually. If contradiction spells progress, syncretism implies stagnation. Contradictions are rational, while syncretism is irra-tional. We have here an application of Marxist categories result-ing in conclusions that echo those of Wittfogel's application of the concept of the Asiatic society to Russia, as well as the earli-est models of "totalitarianism."

What the concept of syncretism conveys therefore is the sharpest, gloomiest, and most desperate critique of Soviet and East European systems yet produced by any Marxist, far more trenchant, more radical, more unsparing than anything written so far either by Yugoslav philosophers or by Eurocommunists. In fact, even though philosophically and methodologically Casals is worlds apart from Solzhenitsyn, their works resemble each other in the force and the comprehensive range of their critique.

As a Marxist, Casals derives the nature of the Soviet social system from its production relations, i.e., from the property relations it has created. He argues, in effect, that the Russian revolution and its subsidiary revolutions in Eastern Europe have destroyed capitalist property but have not succeeded—for complex reasons, which are laid out—in creating a new property system. There is thus a property vacuum, and this in turn spells corresponding voids in all parts of the superstructure, including the withering-away of value, of politics, of the individual personality, of rationality, and of coherence. One mode of production was destroyed, but another was not put in its place; hence this universal vacuosity, held together only by self-perpetuating arbitrariness. In the Theses, Casals summarizes these same results by arguing that the Soviet system mixes (without blending them) an anticapitalist class structure, a capitalist economy, and a feudal state.

The ultimate source of this syncretism is the revolution of 1917, which established a "socialist" regime in a backward society lacking the preconditions Marx and Engels had specified for the transition to socialism. Casals therefore calls Soviet socialism "premature." In turn, the revolution of 1917 brought these results because Leninism differs from Marxism, by being anticipatory rather than obedient to the laws of history. Lenin sought to overcome the deterministic force of these laws, and Stalinism is history's revenge: a prisoner of these same laws, it is condemned to fundamental irrationality. In making statements such as these, Casals by no means seeks to belittle the gigantic achievements made by both Lenin and Stalin, but only to demonstrate their limitations: they have led to a dead end.

The style of these essays is compact, condensed, as if each sentence was the final precipitate of a long thought process. One is reminded of prison notes written under circumstances where paper was in short supply and every word would have to count. The argument is complex, intricate, at times obscure, but always relentless in drawing final conclusions. Each page brings brilliant ideas proffered in provocative formulations. Casals glories in paradoxes and delights in ingenious explanations. This is a dialectical mind seeking to penetrate the ultimate contradictions and incoherencies of Stalinist society and to comprehend it in all its complex ramifications. In presenting these essays to American readers, in a translation by Guy Daniels, I hope they will share the sheer aesthetic delight it has given me to read them. They cannot, I am sure, help being provoked by their messages.

Alfred G. Meyer

The Syncretic Society

INTRODUCTION

Stalinism is often viewed as a power structure that has transformed an economic system. That image is seriously deficient. Stalinism is a force that has transformed an economy by which that force itself has been transformed without realizing it. This retroactive determinism is the basic hypothesis of the present work.

The methodological implication here is plain to see: in adapting itself to the nature of its subject, the study of Stalinism demands an approach on several levels of meaning. The superabundance of narrative detail in the countless biographies and historical studies has built itself up into a veritable saga. Along with the mythology created by Stalinism's defenders, we have had yet another one created by its critics, which likewise does not really tell us much. This kind of research strategy offers more opportunity for venting frustrations than for making discoveries. On the other hand, an analysis centered not on economics or the power structure as such but on *the relations between them*, offers a good chance at setting up theoretical controls for the phenomenon.

This methodological option includes the elements of an initial, general definition of Stalinism as a specific set of relations between the economy and the regime. It also includes a theoretical option indicating Marxism as a system of ideas adapted to the purpose of setting up theoretical controls for Stalinism.

Finally, there is one last problem of general research strategy that must be cleared up from the outset: that of the disciplinary option. For purposes of studying the relations between the economy and the regime, the tools of both political economy and political science are deficient because of their specialization; viz., because of their virtues themselves. A sociological approach seems more amenable to the efforts at synthesis that the subject's ambiguity demands at every step of the way.

The essential thing in Stalinism is the way it organizes ownership of the means of production, and hence production relations. This manner of organization, because of its stability and its unprecedented character, defines Stalinism as an original mode of production. That mode of production arose, not from the débris of capitalism directly after the October Revolution, but from the postrevolutionary and pre-Stalinist society that was in existence for more than a decade. Stalinism is the heir of that society. It was the latter which created the objective and subjective premises for the former's birth. The objective premise was the socioeconomic nature of that intermediate society, while the subjective premise was the theoretical heritage passed on to Stalinism.

For Marx, socialism was to be the result of an objective process advancing inevitably toward the point where the technological character of the productive forces could no longer comport with their social character—their form of capital. This theory assumed as a premise the more or less constant technological development of the productive forces.

Lenin discovered that this premise was lacking in backward countries like Russia. Actually, industrialization was not lagging behind in Russia: it was getting under way, but only sporadically and to the extent demanded by the replication of that lag itself. National capitalism, which in some countries had been the animating force of the industrial revolution, had been transformed into international imperialism, which obstructed industrialization in all the other countries of the world. Blocked by that transformation of capitalism, the task of industrialization had to be taken up by the proletariat. Now it was not industrialization which was leading to socialism, as in Marx, but socialism which was to lead to industrialization. Instead of being a result of the objective process, socialism became its anticipation.

As compared to Marx, the essence of Leninism lay in a double transference. The soil in which socialism germinated was no longer historical necessity but political possibility; and the determining role in its birth was no longer played by the objective process but by subjective strategy; viz., the theoretical subject. The imperialist obstruction of industrialization was converted by Leninism into the premise of an anticipatory revolution, strategic in character. What was at stake in that revolution lay in the realm of the possible: to eliminate the barriers imposed by international imperialism by suppressing national capitalism.

After its triumph, the Leninist revolution did in fact do away with private ownership of the means of production; but it did not eliminate their obsolescence. Thus it implanted a postcapitalist class structure in an economy that was precapitalist as regards the level of its productive forces. It was into this structure that the revolutionary anticipation was incorporated. The latter set aside the social expression of necessity as embodied in the propertied classes, without setting aside the necessity itself as embodied in the underdevelopment of the productive forces. In so doing, it created the concomitance of things that should have been sequential. This combination of pre- and postcapitalist elements makes up the society of premature socialism: premature because of its underdevelopment, socialist because of its unprecedented structure—one liberated from the propertied classes.

Note: According to Marx, the transition from capitalism to socialism would take the form of a historical process in two stages. The first stage would bear the imprint of the capitalist society of which it was the immediate offspring, and which it was supposed to attenuate gradually until it eliminated that imprint. The anticipatory revolution, which modified the general premises of this process, also modified its development. The point of departure for a possible transition to communism was no longer mature capitalism but an underdeveloped capitalism. Thus the two phases foreseen by Marx were preceded by a third one: that of premature socialism. In this phase, presumably, the heritage of underdevelopment in the sphere of productive forces is gradually eliminated along with the organization of production relations, the political system, and the culture, while at the same time, in an anticipatory continuity, the first tasks of the socialist phase are taken on.

The next stage of the transition to communism spontaneously assumed the form of Stalinism, which modified its content. The historic achievement of Stalinism consists in the decisive development of productive forces by the original tactic of anticapitalist and anti-imperialist industrialization. But it is precisely owing to the exclusiveness of that accomplishment that Stalinism has reduced to impoverishment, in a very basic way, the content of the new phase in the process of transition. The elimination of the sequelae of precapitalism in the sphere of the productive forces has been paralleled by their worsening in the spheres of production relations and of political and cultural organization. In combining evolution in one direction with degeneration in others, Stalinism has proven to be a way of perpetuating that unequal development that the Leninist revolution aimed to abolish.

Industrialization excepted, Stalinism has brought about a general replication of underdevelopment in the economy, in politics, and in culture. Summarized in this way, the new phase runs the risk of cutting off all connection with a possible process of transition to socialism. In the long run, Stalinism risks being transformed from a reductive version of premature socialism into its negation. The improvement in the productive forces is itself jeopardized by the atmosphere of general underdevelopment.

From asynchronism, this anticipation passes into structural

incoherence: the socialist class structure and the precapitalist productive forces are incompatible. Although founded on their articulation, premature socialism is a syncretic society.

To a greater extent than the proposed concepts of retroactive determinism, anticipatory revolution, or even premature socialism, that of the syncretic society may provoke very serious objections. For example, one might suppose that it offers a superfluous alternative to that concept so central to the writings of both Hegel and Marx: contradiction. The relation, however, that characterizes syncretism is not contradiction but incompatibility.

The postulate underlying contradiction is unity; that underlying incompatibility is disunity. Contradiction is necessary; incompatibility is merely possible. Contradiction implies polarity—reciprocal conditioning; incompatibility implies relative independence—reciprocal indifference. Contradiction is necessarily dynamic and tends to grow into conflict; incompatibility is normally static and, once established, tends to reproduce itself indefinitely as such. That is why contradiction fosters change, while incompatibility fosters opposition to change. Finally, contradiction stimulates the self-regulating energy of any system, whereas incompatibility opposes a systemic existence, presupposing a regulating energy from without.

Yet none of this means that incompatibility rules out contradiction. Even by virtue of its stabilization, incompatibility has already become a contradiction, because by its very nature, incompatibility—and hence syncretism—is ephemeral and accidental.

Stalinism is precisely that social and economic organization which confers stability on the syncretism engendered by premature socialism. Once achieved, the stabilization of syncretism drifts spontaneously toward inertia. That immobilism is viewed by the proponents of Stalinism as proof of its irreversibility, and by its critics as something willed by a regime that is grimly conservative. In the light of the concept of syncretism, however, that will is itself shown to be objectively conditioned by the nature of the society of which Stalinism is the heir and stabilizer.

That society—premature socialism—discovered that the abolishment of one form of ownership was not followed by the flourishing of another. The latter still had to be created. And it had to meet two equally vital requirements: to be compatible with both the postcapitalist class structure and the precapitalist productive forces, and at the same time, to stimulate (or at least permit) a stepped-up industrialization. All these virtues would make the new form of ownership the objective basis for a gradual advance toward socialism.

In the course of some ten years, premature socialism passed from the prerevolutionary system of ownership through War Communism to the NEP, and finally came to rest on the foundations of the Stalinist mode of production. The last-named involves a kind of ownership that has no historical equivalent. It is convulsive, and marks a definite backward movement from anticipation to hesitation; or in other terms, from the application of a strategy to a search for one. This frantic switching from one form of ownership to another raises a major question: Is premature socialism capable of creating a form of proprietorship that is both adequate and viable? What is in fact at issue here is the theoretical endowment of premature socialism—an aspect that is decisive in understanding Stalinism.

Considered as a theory, Leninism was capable of bringing to birth the society which has posed these problems; but it was not able to solve them. Leninism's radius of action extended no further than the victory of the revolutionary strategy: it gave birth to a society that it did not explain. Thus the first human society to come into being through strategic means, found itself provided with a theory of its birth but lacking a theory for its continued existence.

Yet that missing theory is indispensable. By substituting the possible for the necessary, Leninism engendered a society in which the possible becomes necessary. And such is the case of that theory: the fact of its being necessary derives from the syncretic nature of the society. Any class structure is the projection, on the social plane, of property relations established on the economic plane. Owing to its syncretism, premature socialism tends either to cancel out that relationship in most cases, or to invert it. Now, a class structure cannot create those property relations by which it itself should have been created. The best it can do is to resist their absence with the aid of the relative independence allowed it by syncretism. The anticipated destruction of a form of ownership by strategic means necessitates the creation—also by strategic means—of an alternative form of ownership. The syncretic society makes necessary the subjective action which rendered that society itself possible. In order to be effective with respect to the goals of revolution, that action must be the action of a theoretical subject.

The paradox which combines the imperative need for, and the absence of, a theory of premature socialism is programmed into the genetic code of Stalinism. Disarmed in the face of that absence, Stalinism yields to that imperative by founding its legitimacy on the supposed monopoly of a theory that is inaccessible to it. In order to give itself a social existence, the theory masquerades as a kind of personal providence. The theoretical subject becomes a mythological subject. The general human faculty of reflection becomes a vocation that is superhuman and hence unique. The socialization of an adequate theory is replaced by a coercive ideology rendered private to an extreme degree. All this is the work of Stalinism, which, in transforming the act of reflection into an act of power, has substituted the theory's interdiction for its inherited inaccessibility.

The evolution of the theory produces one of the most distinct dissociations between premature socialism and Stalinism. It was premature socialism which posed the theory in its three essential aspects: that of generative force, of legitimizing necessity, and of absence. To this, Stalinism added its own contribution, consisting in the absorption of theory by power. In this way, legitimacy becomes identity: embodied in one and the same providential leader, theory and power become identical. At that moment, the theory becomes as indisputable as the power. As the sole possessor of the theory, the power is naturally not subject to any checks. That which is legitimized in this way is no longer the society but the fact that the power is not subject to any checks. The strength of this structure depends on the coherence of its irrationalism. It is because of that coherence that the providential leader is able to fulfill his function: to convert the theoretical vacuum into a legitimizing theory.

Stalinism makes irreversible that temporary lack of theory that it inherited. A legitimacy of this kind is indispensable to this type of social organization. The glorification and perpetuation of the failure of theory only seems to be paradoxical. In that failure, of which it was both cause and consequence, Stalinism glorifies and perpetuates itself. In the transition from premature socialism to Stalinism, a society committed to overcoming necessity comes to be dominated by the latter in one of its most oppressive forms. Stalinism's alienation from premature socialism derives from the former's fraudulent response to the specific necessity of the theoretical subject.

Stalinism's failure with respect to socialism has been concomitant with its success in the matter of industrialization. Although limited, that success is of great historical scope: it confirms the Leninist assumption that the suppression of national capitalism would allow the backward countries to rid themselves of international imperialism's opposition to their industrialization. It does not, however, confirm another Leninist assumption: that anticapitalist and antisocialist industrialization could be converted, as it progressed, into a gradual transition towards socialism. In unleashing industrialization, Stalinism bowed to the harshest necessity; in failing to steer that process (in advance) in the direction of socialism, Stalinism abandoned the most revolutionary possibility.

This reversal of Leninism—the abandonment of the possible in favor of necessity—forms the subject of a postulate fundamental to Stalinism's fraudulence [*mystification*] on the theoretical plane. That postulate confuses anticapitalist industrialization with the construction of socialism. It suggests that in the absence of capitalism, industrialization spontaneously "secretes" socialism. The theoretical subject becomes the historical object: it abandons to an illusory spontaneity a task that can be accomplished only by a strategy elaborated theoretically, and one that it is incapable of—the strategy of the socialist integration of industrialization's gains.

The basic reduction of socialism to industrialization is merely the outward expression of an entire chain of reductions that led up to the former: from theory to power, from possibility to necessity, from strategy to spontaneity. If one separates the elements of these pairs that have been rendered illusory, one can see that, far from being a theory which bases a strategy of socialist transition on the ground of the possible, Stalinism is nothing more than a power structure expressing spontaneously the need for industrialization.

Stalinism does not act *on* necessity, but in its name. Such is its basis for solving the fundamental problem left unsolved by premature socialism: that of organizing ownership, the decisive premise of industrialization. That organization consists largely in the productive utilization and multiplication of the means of production, whose form of ownership is essential to this process. The convulsive form of ownership that was typical of premature socialism had defined the terms of the problem: the premature but effective elimination of the private ownership of the means of production creates the risk of establishing their premature but ineffective social ownership. Being intolerable in its private mode, and inaccessible in its social form, ownership becomes volatile.

Stalinism did not create this ownership-in-abeyance. Rather, it represents an economic and social system which is centered not on a transition of that state of abeyance toward social ownership but on the former's perpetuation. Having acquired an historical existence because of its duration, ownership-in-abeyance must also acquire a conceptual existence. It is quite possible that such a role could be assumed by the formula of a property vacuum. In the light of that concept, Stalinism can be viewed as a mode of production based on a system of organizing ownership which is doubly negative: anticapitalist (because capitalism has been eliminated) and nonsocialist (because social ownership was never tried out). Those interpretations which attribute to proprietorship under Stalinism a univocal and/or positive character overlook the essential uniqueness of that multivocal society.

At first glance, the concept of a vacuum of ownership makes for a certain distrust. It represents, however, phenomena that are perfectly familiar from the historical viewpoint but overlooked from the conceptual viewpoint; e.g., the land reform that followed the October Revolution. Promulgated by the Second Congress of Soviets after the take-over of the Winter Palace, the Land Decree proclaimed that land was ". . . a national patrimony put in the possession of those who worked it." Land ownership was made completely vague: control was separated from possession. One historian of the USSR has rightly stated that ". . . the Land Decree introduced a principle that was quite the opposite of ownership in rural areas" (Hélène Carrère d'Encausse, *L'Union Soviétique de Lénine à Staline: 1917-1953*, p. 77). The concept of a property vacuum is aimed at grasping the phenomenon while avoiding its definition by negation.

The property vacuum represents the absence of autonomous economic mechanisms securing for one social stratum the complete ownership, juridically ratified, of the means of production. Complete proprietorship makes it possible to control both the organization of production and the appropriation of the product. In this sense, the absence of proprietors is the best proof of a property vacuum. The latter consists in an incomplete control of the prerogatives of ownership; viz., a control limited to organizing production. As such, it results not from the action of an autonomous economic mechanism but from a perpetual extra-economic intervention. Finally, it is not ratified juridically, since laws can legitimize ownership but not its absence. That is why, under Stalinism, law does not merely proclaim ownership: it supplants the latter.

Under the conditions of a property vacuum, the means of production can neither be sold nor bought: they are not commodities. Consequently, they do not have an economically determined value. Yet they do have a conventional price—one intended to serve only the purposes of accounting. That noneconomic price is assigned to them, necessarily, by an extra-economic authority possessing that prerogative. The production of means of production is not aimed at their profitable sale. Hence the mechanism of its regulation is not the economic stimulus of a viable demand but an extra-economic order [*commande*] : the plan. For Stalinist industrialization, this substitution of an order for demand plays an essential role. That is why it becomes, spontaneously, the general model for organizing social relations.

The property vacuum has the result that the means of production are shifted into an extra-economic sphere. This means that they are not susceptible of appropriation, since ownership does not exist outside the economic sphere. Thus the means of production have a real existence as regards technology, and only an apparent existence as economic phenomena.

According to the Stalinist dispensation, the means of production are owned by the producers themselves. According to most of Stalinism's critics, the means of production are owned by the State or the bureaucracy. Although it dismisses both of these assertions, the concept of a property vacuum does not equate them with each other. First, there is already an important equalizing element: the two categories of presumptive owners share in the appropriation of the social product via the same mechanism, the wage. (Here one must except collectivized agriculture.) This form of appropriation—which is indirect, nonspecific, and independent of the appropriating subject—does not confirm, in economic terms, the proprietary character ascribed to the two categories. The elements of their inequality do not involve the amount of salary but rather its connection with the work done, and the degree to which ownership is inaccessible to them. The incomplete control of certain prerogatives of ownership, which is typical of a property vacuum, remains strictly inaccessible to the producers, and constitutes a monopoly of power. Hence it is solely with respect to that monopoly that the property vacuum is manifested as a separation between the possession and control of property. The monopoly, therefore, is not one of ownership but of its incomplete control founded on nonpossession.

The limits to this incomplete control are set by the common form of appropriation: the wage. Hence there is a lack of connection between the nature of that activity and its remuneration, which engenders yet another nonrelation: between the amount of activity and the amount of remuneration.

This brings us to the second inequality between the two categories. Although equalized by the mode common to both, the wage, they are differentiated by the varied action of that common mode. If one is willing to apply the term "management" to the incomplete control of property, one can state that the general principle "to each according to his work" applies to the nonmanagerial producers but not to the managers, who are not producers. From this angle of vision, the latter are also favored as compared to capitalists, since profits express precisely the dependence of appropriation on the economic results of management.

In the monopoly of management, Stalinism has created a specific type of activity without at the same time creating a specific mechanism for its remuneration. In so doing, it has provided the objective basis for the separation between management and responsibility. Lacking any economic standard of comparison, managerial activity is subject to no audit on the social plane. The fact that it is protected against any regular economic penalty represents the economic basis of its infallibility. A system of management which is unaffected either by production or by its economic valuation, is in fact not subject to any evaluation. Thus infallibility expresses, not an evaluation of the managers' abilities, but the society's systematic inability to evaluate this kind of activity. Perfection being incommensurable, the incommensurable is perceived as perfection. This attribute is possessed, not by the different individuals performing a certain function, but by the function performed by those different individuals.

After a while the property vacuum, being artificially maintained, engenders the objective necessity of this subjectification: the function of infallibility. Criticism of Stalinism on the level of the "cult of personality" only perpetuates the confusion between the objective necessity for that function in a property vacuum and the historical agents who perform that function at one time or another. Actually, all those figures who lose that function—whether through death or political change—lose at the same time that infallibility which they personified without possessing it. The function of infallibility perdures, regardless of those ephemeral figures who perform it, and who are usually found, *a posteriori*, to have been personally unfit to fulfill that function. It is not the providential leaders who produce the function of infallibility: it is the function of infallibility which produces the agglomeration of providential leaders. The true message brought by the providential leader is that of a society dominated by providence; i.e., by the most tyrannical form of necessity: chance, which is the natural result of failure in the matter of theory. The infallible leader is the institutionalized negation of theory, although he claims to be its sole incarnation. But the best that theory can do is to be adequate. The moment it is declared infallible, it is already dead, having degenerated into mythology.

The result is an evident confusion of values of which the infallible leader is only one of the consequences. Its most general consequence is incommensurability, which spontaneously gives rise to a lack of proportionality [*démesure*].* The latter represents the lack of a system of values that is coherent, adequate, and hence socially operative. Such a system can unify elements that are diverse yet mutually conditioned. It cannot, however, unify elements that are disjunct by reason of their incompatibility. The syncretism of the society is echoed in the syncretism of its values.

It is via the property vacuum that the lack of proportionality—a fruitful concept for the study of Stalinism—comes into being. It is in disproportion that the need for measure and its inaccessibility come together. Lack of proportionality is the absence of criteria, or their illegitimate application. It therefore represents the distorted satisfaction of the need for measure. "By its very nature," wrote Marx, "law cannot exist without the application of a regular unit of measure." The lack of such a standard measure renders law itself irregular; i.e., unequally binding. Whatever is placed beyond the measurable is also outside of the law.

The property vacuum represents the only modern organization of propietorship that is not legally ratified. Thus the determining social relation is outside of the law. Stalinist law legitimizes a form of ownership which, being a plan, is not a reality, so that the first-named necessarily ignores the real status of ownership. At the same time, the law puts itself in the realm of the unreal, and puts the fundamental reality of ownership in a clandestine status. In creating and perpetuating this cleavage, Stalinist law condemns itself to general ineffectiveness. In a Stalinist society, as in any other, weaknesses in the law provoke excesses on the part of the regime. As an expression of the lack of proportionality, the excessive authority is incarnated in the incommensurable and infallible leader.

*Casals seems to be using *démesure* (a rather arcane word) in overlapping senses, to suggest both a lack of proportionality and immeasurability.—G.D.

The incommensurable becomes the measurer for all activities not its own. It ordains disproportionality in the form of measures which, although theoretically undemonstrable, must be indisputable on the practical plane. The chief indicators of this inverted lack of proportionality are the tempo of industrialization, the rate of accumulation, the disarticulation among sectors of the economy, the price of labor power, the price of means of production, the goals of the plan, the degree of separation between decision making and production, the forms taken by the ideological affirmation of the measuring authority's infallibility, etc. The "subjectification" of these decisive measures reveals this social system's incapacity for self-regulation.

In its price, labor power exhibits a double appearance: that of its sale and that of its value. Placed in a context where its value is debased, labor power has no other means of reproducing itself than its price. Through the loss of its value and the preservation of its price, its measurement is rendered at once indispensable and unrealizable. As a vestige of a system of measurement that has been eliminated, the price of labor power expresses another. The content of that price is not its value as determined by the objective mechanisms of the economy but its valuation as fixed by the subjective decisions of the regime.

From this angle of vision, one system of values is expressed in the units of measure of another. This confusion is a sign of disproportionality, which is also to be found, therefore, in the way labor power is regulated. The very real disjuncture between the latter's value and its price creates an objective necessity for a subjective evaluator of labor power. Thus the lack of proportionality becomes general but not equal. It affects both the power structure and the workers, but with contrary results. Owing to the absence of proportionality, the power structure is above all measurement: the incommensurable becomes inestimable—infallible. Owing to that same immeasurability [*démesure*], labor power is situated not above all measure but outside of all measure proper to it. Here the incommensurable becomes susceptible of evaluation—the object of a subjective appraisal.

Thus the hold that this quality of immeasurability has over the regime is different from that which it has over the workers; and this fact accounts for its twofold character. It spares the regime from any measurement, and it subjects labor power to inadequate measurement. This inequality in the matter of immeasurability is a basic characteristic of the Stalinist mode of production. Manifested solely as infallibility, the disproportion of the power structure cannot but be recognized by the workers. Manifested solely as inadequate measurement, disproportionality as applied to the latter can have only the power structure as its source. Thus the inequality does not involve dimensions but roles: evaluation operates in one direction only. All the economic, political, and ideological techniques exclude any real evaluation of the regime by the workers, and make the last-named dependent upon their evaluation by the regime. In this sense, the subject and the object of disproportionality separate. Exempt from all measurement, and being, at the same time, the general dispenser of disproportion, the power structure knows no bounds.

The objective reality of a property vacuum coupled with the separation between labor and management, engenders an objective necessity for a vacuum of measurement. The debasement of the value of labor power creates an objective necessity for its subjective evaluation. In taking on this role, the regime is not lending itself to an abuse; it is simply conforming to a necessity of which it is unaware and which therefore dominates it.

It does not suffice that this role be assumed by those who are supposed to fill it: it must also be made acceptable to those who are supposed to bear its consequences. In order to be acceptable, the evaluations dispensed by the regime should be fair. That requirement is just as reasonable as it is impossible to meet. It is this impossibility of providing only fair evaluations that renders the regime infallible. In order to be functional in this respect, the latter must be situated not above all error but above all judgment.

As organized by Stalinism, the property vacuum demands

the kind of disproportionality that in turn demands infallibility. This disproportion, *qua* infallibility, serves as the instrument of disproportion *qua* the noneconomic price of labor power—with all its consequences.

Before becoming a power structure that knows no bounds, Stalinism is the mode of production that engenders the former by combining, on the one hand, the property vacuum with the separation between labor and management and, on the other, the debasement of the value of labor power with the necessity of its nonnegotiable sale.

To insist on the objective conditioning of the power structure under Stalinism is by no means tantamount to underestimating the immense role played by subjective and circumstantial factors. Indeed, the distorted image of Stalinism is a result, more than anything else, of a unilateral approach from the other direction. To reduce Stalinism to subjective and circumstantial factors is to beg the question as to why the providential leaders come and go, whereas the Stalinist society perdures. Those who do so, project onto Stalinism the anticipatory and strategic nature of its revolutionary origins. But the ultimately decisive factor in the evolution of Stalinism is not its origins but rather its economy. Stalinism strays far from this fundamental postulate of Marxism—and hence from an understanding of itself—when it ascribes that decisive role to the regime. But the latter can assign that indeterminate and all-determining role to itself only by seeking its *raison d'être* in the realm of the irrational.

The image of the indeterminate nature of the regime is the logical complement of its lack of proportionality and its role as general evaluator. This transfer of the measurement of all activities from an impersonal mechanism to a personified power structure confers upon the Stalinist economy an arbitrary character [*caractère d'octroi*] that is transmitted to the entire society. The historical model for the command economy—and hence for the mandating authority—is offered by feudalism.

Arbitrary command [*l'octroi*], in this sense, is the nonnegotiable, nonegalitarian distribution—not subject to audit—of scarcity by the direct use of force. Because of this role played by force, in command societies war is not "the extension of politics by other means." Rather, war and politics merge.

The command economy is a suitable substitute for a competitive economy, as well as for a self-regulating one. Thus it is an adequate solution for the stabilization of the property vacuum. Under capitalism, the mode of distribution is the basis of power. In a command economy, power becomes the basis for the mode of distribution. That is why, in such an economy, production relations function as relations of force.

The generalization of command is the mirror image of the generalization of interdiction. The essential mechanism of the command economy is the arbitrary—hence prohibitive—authority. The chief instrument of that authority is force, either potential or actual. This explains why that authority is at once extra-economic and extrapolitical. Because of that double exteriority, arbitrariness is not confined to any particular sphere: it extends to the entire society. Thus the arbitrary authority is not exercised in either the economic or the political domain but in the social order. Under these conditions, the social order is manifested above all in the stability of, and a respect for, commands. And the stability and respectability of those commands are a direct function of the stability and respectability of the arbitrary authority.

In order to make the transient perdurable, the social order is transformed into social inertia [*immobilité*]. And it is for the purpose of effecting that transformation, that the arbitrary authority becomes an infallible authority; that the infallible authority becomes an infallible personage; and that the infallible personage becomes the commander. The decisions of the personified arbitrary authority are perfect not because of their merits but because of their source. Here we find empiricism functioning in its purest state: the correctness of a decision is proved by the fact that it was made. It is not an odd bunch of exceptionally gifted persons who reproduce the institution of the infallible leader who is the commander. Rather, it is the command economy which reproduces the necessity for an infallible leader, without any special regard for the gifts of those who are candidates for that function. Like their biographers, those whom chance designates to play this necessary role ascribe to themselves virtues that actually belong to the function.

On the ruins of inequality as expressed in private ownership, Stalinism erects inequality as expressed in arbitrary allocations. These new relations of inequality are characterized by their rigidity, their transparence, and their omnipresence. The institution of the infallible leader is the general symbol of that inequality. The exceptional nature of infallibility implies that fallibility is the rule. Any exceptional individual other than the leader breaks that rule: hence the intolerance toward great artists, scientists, etc. This water-tight partitioning includes in its principle the general negation of real individuals in favor of an illusory individual. As organized by Stalinism, the property vacuum also becomes a vacuum of individuals—one projected onto a symbolic being who is necessarily superhuman.

History proves that command societies are not political in nature. The same incompatibility is found in the Stalinist society. There, exercising power means rejecting discussion, negotiation, competition, and compromise—viz., those means which are essentially political—so that the result is a depolitization of power manifested in the constant use of direct coercion. At the other pole of inequality, the same decline in political relations is manifested in the political inertia of the masses. The rhetoric of coercion, which is that of the power structure, is from time to time echoed by the masses. In the Stalinist society, the mainly politicized class struggles characteristic of capitalism are replaced by explosive, sporadic riots of a kind characteristic of precapitalist societies. The metamorphosis of the political power structure into a regime based on arbitrary command is the most potent manifestation of the former's conditioning. The coercive function, which capitalism transmitted unstintingly to the mechanics of the economy, is retrieved on no less a scale, under Stalinism, by the mechanics of power. This functional change engenders a corresponding mutation in the power structure manifested in predominance of the military and police organization over political organization properly so-called.

The management of the economy is put into the hands of an authority that exists outside the economy. That authority rules out the economic valuation of its management of the economy. Not only does it prevent economic mechanisms from producing the system of measures proper to them, but it obliges those mechanisms to lend an appearance of economically plausible measures to the disproportions that it imposes on the economy. Since the control of property, as a vacuum, cannot be founded on a specific economic mechanism, it is founded on the mechanism that is most specifically meta-economic: the power structure.

The disproportionality imposed by the meta-economic authority takes on the appearance of proportion produced by economic mechanisms. The specific ambiguity of the economy and of the power structure expresses, in its own way, the general syncretism of the society. Before becoming a privilege, the regime's ability to make its decisions economically plausible is a consequence of the property vacuum. When perpetuated, the latter has only one result; namely, to "diseconomize" the very foundation of the economy: property. Being a link between the economic and the meta-economic spheres, the property vacuum can reproduce itself only by institutionalizing its own ambiguity: that of an extra-economic mechanism which regulates the economy. Thus the regime's function of managing the economy directly, is economically determined. Its enormous power does not derive from its specific traits but from the imperative generated by the perpetuation of the property vacuum. The latter models not only the necessity for an extra-economic authority regulating the economy from the outside but also the most important parameters of that authority's functioning.

Any proprietorship of the means of production is a discretionary power masquerading as an economic prerogative. The property vacuum does away with that masquerade. The control of property conceals its precapitalist form of the transparent exercise of power. The equality latent in the generalized absence of ownership becomes a manifest inequality materialized in the monopoly of power. The nondistribution of ownership is buttressed by the nondistribution of power, generally labeled "centralization."

The regime rules out the possibility of being conditioned by a form of ownership of which it thinks itself to be the creator. It assumes it is holding that conditioning under control in reproducing it. Under Stalinism, society gets away from the dominion of one kind of necessity only to fall under that of another.

Given the property vacuum, the growing mass of the means of production imposes a specific function upon society: the function of supervision. This development is strongly fostered by the immobilism of the regime, the relative vacuum of legality, and the scarcity of consumer goods. The modification of the relations among these different factors entails a modification of the priorities of the supervisory function. Although at first it is applied mostly to the material factors of production, it later takes as its chief object the human factors of that same process. This is a result of industrialization, which in this way makes for the multiplication and dispersion not only of material factors but of the production apparatus. The shift is due to the separation between the producers and the means of production. Under these conditions, the exercise of supervision becomes part and parcel of the control of property—a prerogative that seriously aggravates the separation between the regime and the producers.

Such a separation gives rise to two contrary developments. As industrialization advances, the production apparatus tends toward ever wider dispersion, to the point of atomization, while the supervisory authority tends to shrink to the point of person-ification. In order to avoid this opposition, it would seem that one should either impart to the production apparatus the cen-tralizing tendency of the regime, or impart to the regime the contrary tendency of the apparatus. But Stalinism resorts to a third solution: creating an enormous segment of society whose function it is to keep watch on the rest of society. This bureau-cracy, which some authors call "the new class," is thus a direct result of the property vacuum. Through its existence, the separa-tion between the regime and the producers assumes concrete form on the societal plane. Whether or not it is actually a class, the bureaucracy thus makes for the erosion of that class struc-ture that it should have defended. In this way, the function of constantly producing socially operative disproportionality creates for itself a suitable structure, itself out of proportion. The disproportionateness of the bureaucracy is manifested in its size, in the multitude of its prerogatives, and in the fact that it is not subject to audit, thus reflecting the primary infallibility that is served by it. The bureaucracy is one of the fundamental proofs of the strong hold that the precapitalist model has on Stalinism. As a matter of fact, it is a replica of an old form of the division of labor—one whereby the nonproducers keep tab on the producers. The specific task assigned to it under Stalin-ism is to make supervision possible while yet preserving the opposition between the dispersion of production and the centralization of political power.

As the mediator between these opposite trends, the Stal-inist bureaucracy cannot in the long run avoid its own break-down: that contingent of bureaucrats which has joined forces with the interests of the production units comes into conflict with the one connected directly with the Center. The centraliza-tion of political power involves the systematic destructuraliza-tion of the other social entities and institutions. Under Stalin-ism, the production units are the only institutions that cannot be weakened in any essential way by this process of destructuralization. In other words, they are the only social entities capable of founding their own interests on a structure possessing a certain degree of autonomy. It is because of these solid foundations that the polarization mentioned above causes the erosion of the presumptive mediator between the opposite trends.

Under Stalinism, the cleavage of the bureaucracy is mainly manifested in a struggle for information. The supervisory function becomes a technique of distortion. In becoming a vacuum of information, the property vacuum takes on a material identity. Productive capacities whose physical existence is without flaw, become economically nonexistent. The breakdown of the bureaucracy is accompanied by that of its function: supervision becomes a matter of deceit on the one hand and mistrust and coercion on the other.

Being divided against itself at the basic level of interests, the Stalinist bureaucracy can hardly be considered a social class, much less a ruling class.

The property vacuum models not only the organization of political power but also that of the production relations, which are determinants for the Stalinist mode of production, just as they are for any other.

The property vacuum sets the generalized inaccessibility of the possession of property off against the strict monopoly of its incomplete control. In this way the economic foundation is laid for the separation between management and labor. It is under the decisive impact of that separation that the production relations characteristic of Stalinism are formed.

Liberated from capital and endowed with a kind of ownership that is inoperative, the producers again find themselves under the economic compulsion of selling their labor power. This point is essential to production relations of the Stalinist type, since the necessity of selling labor power is coupled with a prohibition against buying it. The monopoly of the incomplete control of ownership is transformed into a monopoly of the right to buy labor power. The extra-economic authority—in this case, the State—becomes the sole employer.

Labor power remains a commodity. For its possessor, its only use-value is its exchangeability. But that exchange is blocked by the lack of juridically equal parties who own commodities of a different kind that they would like to exchange for labor power. Thus the labor market is reduced to a mere seeming existence, similar to that of ownership. The formal equality between the parties to an exchange is replaced not by a real equality but by a general inequality, both real and formal. On one side are the producers, who have only their labor power at their disposal. On the other side is the State as employer—an employer who not only has the power of making decisions about the means of production but is competent to dictate, via legal regulations, the behavior of the other parties to the transaction, the producers. These production relations combine two kinds of inequality: economic inequality, like that of capitalism, and juridical inequality, like that of precapitalist modes of production.

The result is the elimination of those conditions which make the process of buying and selling labor power a negotiable one. The sham market for the buying of labor power becomes the site of its bogus sale. The nonnegotiable regulation of labor power is a determining factor not in production relations but in the entirety of social relations. This is why Stalinism may be rightly defined as a nonnegotiable or nontransactional society.

The generalized nonnegotiability casts doubts on the usefulness of those institutions whose function it is to negotiate. The functional atrophy which afflicts the trade organizations of the producers is inscribed in the logic of this kind of relations. The first-named also makes for mutations in the nature of the party of the working class. The general erosion of class organizations—something that has often been remarked—is currently ascribed to a stratagem of the regime. In moving in that direction, however, the regime is merely conforming to the imperatives of the production relations characteristic of an economy in which the stabilized property vacuum is coupled with a strict separation between producers and management. Thus Stalinism is reconstructing, *a posteriori* and by means of anticapitalist economy, the original disorganization of the proletariat that nascent capitalism built, *a priori*, by means of its own economy.

Mature capitalism proved compatible with the consolidation of workers' organizations. That development had an economic foundation: capital could not dominate labor power without truly converting it into a commodity. That marketable reality is the reality of exchange, and hence of the negotiability of its sale. Under Stalinism both the sale of labor power and its marketability are spurious. Workers' organizations, indispensable to real exchange, only encumber sham exchange. Here the producers' alienation *vis-à-vis* the means of production includes alienation *vis-à-vis* their own organizations. The latter are not suppressed, but their functions are inverted. Their dysfunction with respect to their initial goals makes these organizations fit to perform their specific function under Stalinism: to make sure that the buying and selling of labor power is nonnegotiable.

The property vacuum creates an organizational vacuum for itself. In order to be economically operative, nonnegotiability also takes root in politics. Via this extension, the nonnegotiability of the price of labor power becomes a particular case of the general nonnegotiability of the decisions regulating all of societal life. There are no two ways about it: the indisputable remains, by its very nature, asocial. That is why its need to take on an air of legitimacy also tends toward the asocial in the specific form of the superhuman. An essential aspect of this metamorphosis, therefore, is the personification of decision making: the indisputable nature of the decisions reflects the infallibility of the decision maker. Power becomes personal because infallibility cannot be collectivized. The only way the infallible can aspire to becoming plausible is by remaining unique —the exceptional result of a stroke of luck. The repository of personal power becomes a providential personage. As this role becomes institutional, so does the extinction of debate. Any real dialogue would be a challenge to the very principle of infallibility. If he agreed to a real discussion with fallible people, the infallible one would be acknowledging them as his equal. It is almost a tautology to note that discussion is the manifest negation of the indisputable. Thus that political freak, infallibility, proves to be the mythologizing legitimacy of a mechanism essential to Stalinist production relations: the nonnegotiable employment of labor power.

The generalized absence of discussion takes the form of a system of ratifying organizations and institutions. This system fulfills a function much more important than merely simulating a nonexistent democracy: it assures that indisputability will be everywhere enforced. In so doing, it creates a social, political, and cultural ambiance capable of making the nonnegotiable sale of labor power plausible and even normal. It is because of this prevalence of nondialogue—or, if you will, of the "decisional monologue"—that Stalinism taken as a whole becomes a nontransactional society.

The thoroughly backward character of Stalinist society is, in the last analysis, due to the kind of property ownership and production relations that are peculiar to it. That character is made especially plain in the way it organizes political power, and in its ideology. With its concentration on anticapitalism, Stalinism seems to overlook the largely precapitalist nature of the society whose heir it is, and whose deep imprint it bears. It is under the burden of that disregarded origin that Stalinism has managed to avoid the restoration of capitalist private ownership, by establishing production relations that are for the most part precapitalist. To put it more precisely, Stalinism is the elimination of precapitalism as regards production technology, founded on an anticapitalist form of ownership and a precapitalist pattern for organizing production relations and political power. The roots of this precapitalism are, for the most part, to be found in the regime's economic functions: the direct use of extra-economic coercion in regulating production relations.

The nonnegotiated and nonnegotiable conditions of employment take the form of a contract that is legally guaranteed. Thus the law is further weakened: it sanctions the contractual —and hence transactional—character of a relation that is regulated in a univocal and coercive manner. Along with a proprietorship that is of no real validity, the law accords the producers a competency to negotiate that is illusory. At the same time, it ignores the dominant reality of univocal decision making as regards the distribution, the price, and the basic conditions of utilization of labor power.

The general function of univocal decision making consists in basing industrialization on the systematic victimization of the producers. The separation between management and workers transforms a possible voluntary sacrifice into one that is imposed. The restrictive satisfaction of the producers' needs permits the stimulative satisfaction of production's needs. The nonnegotiability of employment has the aim of expanding production by reducing consumption. The general orientation toward this goal is expressed in a veritable principle of the Stalinist economy: a lack of balance [*déséquilibre*] among the sectors.

The lasting realization of the relation $A > B$ is conditioned by a distribution of labor power adapted to that relation. This unbalanced distribution of socially necessary labor represents a twofold ignorance *vis-à-vis* its traditional regulator: a viable demand for the products of each sector. What makes it possible is the existence of the extra-economic authority which has a monopoly on employment. Channeled toward Sector A by virtue of this monopoly, a large part of the labor power produces means of production that do not correspond to any viable demand. The economic illegitimacy of these products is transferred to the labor power expended on their production. In strictly economic terms, this labor is not socially necessary.

Now, according to Marx, socially necessary labor represents

the substance of value. Any labor that is not of this kind is not productive of value and hence devoid of value itself. Thus the economic system of value has rotted at the core. The value of all products—and that of labor power above all—becomes economically incommensurable. Price cannot be the measure of a value that is itself debased. The function of the former consists in attributing to immeasurability the form of its negation. The objective foundation of disproportionality is the debasement of value brought about by the economically nonproductive use of a part of the labor power. Labor's material productivity is separated from its economic productivity. In such a case, only one of two things can happen to price: it can be abolished, or it can be determined by extra-economic decision making. Deprived of the reality of its value, labor power is subjected to the reality of an unreal price which constitutes the perfectly real condition of its reproduction. Physical production is liberated from economic productivity. Put into the service of industrialization, the production relations transfer their own nature to the former. Immeasurability, which makes infallibility inevitable, also makes possible an industrialization obsessed with production and indifferent to value.

The twofold character of the price of labor power—real and unreal—remains beyond the grasp of the producers. Its unreality as a measure of value remains imperceptible to them beyond its reality as the only means of reproducing their labor power. Because of this flawed perception, when the producers sell their labor power and get a wage as payment for it, they believe they are in the economic domain of exchange. But in fact they are in the extra-economic domain of political power. The nonnegotiable employment of labor power represents not a relation of exchange but one of domination. Production relations are absorbed by power relations. However, in preserving basic economic mechanisms to which they assign specific functions, the production relations manifest themselves, for the most part, as economic relations.

This *quid pro quo* conceals a fundamental substitution:

the decisions of the regime replace the law of value, but not its system of measurement. An objective system of measurement is destroyed before the necessity for it has been obviated. In this fact we see the consequences of the original anticipation. Stalinism is the definite rejection of one economic system of values coupled with the inability to build another. The impersonal, objective measurement of each person's activity is replaced by measurement that is personified, hence subjective and nonsystematic. This authoritarian, noneconomic allocation of resources has made possible a real historical mutation: the industrial take-off. Stalinism is not to be condemned for having introduced this technique but for having made it immutable, and for having thus transformed a mode of transition into a mode of production. In this process, the desystematization of measurement results from the transformation of the power of value into the value of power.

The dissolution of production relations into power relations has been due chiefly to the replacement of measures resulting from economic laws by measures resulting from decisions by the regime that have juridical force. The measures imposed by the regime have the general characteristic of immeasurability. Immeasurability is tantamount to a private evaluation of specific criteria, extremely subjective, based on a legitimacy that is irrational and hence socially indisputable and not subject to audit, and expressed in the terms of a system that it rejects, thereby creating a general confusion of values. Thus the uncontrolled vacuum of ownership leads to a vacuum of measurement.

The direct regulation of production relations by means of extra-economic compulsion has the result that they become subjectivized. Under conditions of a general nonnegotiability, that process is manifested as the personal dependence of all the producers on the sole employer. All these distinctly backward traits endow the Stalinist economy with the character of an anticapitalism of the precapitalist type. Production relations of this kind subject the industrial worker, at one and the same time, to economic compulsion and extra-economic coercion; and these two things merge to a point where one cannot be distinguished from the other.

The economic form of what passes as wages is not content to abandon its specific content. It takes on a different, nonspecific content to which it lends all the importance of specificity. Nonnegotiated wages fixed by an extra-economic decision represent that form, which is at once fraudulent and effective. It confers the compulsory force of objective economic laws upon the coercive subjectivity of the decision makers.

The extra-economic coercion is not replaced by economic compulsion but rather amplified by it. In deciding how labor power is to be allocated and remunerated, the extra-economic coercion also endows the practical process of labor with its coercive character. The nonnegotiable regulation of labor power makes it possible, on the basis of a coercive organization of labor, for anticapitalist industrialization to take off. What was conjectural becomes irreversible: the industrial take-off becomes a thing of the past, but the coercive organization of labor remains, and even worsens. Coercive labor represents an objective tendency determined by the existence of production relations that are doubly coercive. Forced labor is a subjective hyperbolization going beyond that objective tendency. Coercive labor is inherent in Stalinist production relations. Forced labor is a further development of those same relations that is always possible under the impact of circumstantial and psychological factors. Such being the case, to characterize Stalinism by using the symbol of the Gulag, is to conceal its basic nature under its accidental aspects. At different times, Stalinism has proved itself able to exist without forced labor, but never without coercive labor. The condition of dependence does not need an incarcerated worker in order to be effective: a worker at liberty suffices.

Since it is sold on a sham market, labor power can acquire the means for its reproduction only by observing very strictly the rules of a real market: that of the means of subsistence. The syncretism of the society emerges as the existential double of the worker, who is compelled to live both in the world of the economy and in that of the meta-economic. The economic essence of Stalinism is revealed in the worker's double life. In order to eliminate its inherited syncretism, Stalinism unleashed accelerated industrialization. In order to achieve accelerated industrialization, Stalinism is aggravating that inherited syncretism which makes up content of the production relations.

Owing to the property vacuum, the general syncretism of that society does more than just survive: it penetrates into the foundations of the economy, engendering syncretic production relations. Their character does not consist in the parallel existence of different kinds of production relations, but in their fusion. Stalinist production relations represent the stabilized interlocking of elements of production relations that are mutually incompatible. In this pluralistic situation, as in any other, theory seeks a dominant element. For the Stalinist ideology, that dominant element is socialist. For certain critics of Stalinism, it is capitalist, reducing Stalinism to the status of one particular variety of state capitalism. The two definitions are equally vulnerable, having recourse to one and the same procedure—that of their reciprocal omission. Actually, Stalinist production relations combine elements proper to socialism, to capitalism, and especially to precapitalism—the last-named being those most overlooked by the analysts. The search for some dominant element among these production relations includes in its premises an ignorance of their essence; viz., their syncretism.

Stalinist production relations are socialist in that they effectively rule out the private ownership of the means of production, the private buying of labor power, and hence the private accumulation of the surplus product.

Stalinist production relations are capitalist—and even monopolist—in that they maintain the economic compulsion of the sale of labor power which is supposed to produce a maximum increment value, both absolute and relative, whose utilization is not subject to audit by its creator.

Stalinist production relations are precapitalist in that they base the regulating of labor power on the nonnegotiability of the conditions. In such relations, economic compulsion is coupled with extra-economic coercion, which leads to a coercive organization of labor.

This organic eclecticism of the production relations has made possible an industrial expansion followed by slow but discernible improvement in several areas: great social mobility; stepped-up urbanization; increased consumption (the underconsumption of the industrial worker being superior to that in the village he has just left); no owner-bosses, unemployment, or the threat of such; access to education at all levels; better medical care; unlimited opportunities for advancement for one's children; etc. These considerable advantages are of course accompanied by the kinds of servitude mentioned above.

The chief economic result of the combination of a coercive organization of labor and underconsumption, is chronic underproductivity. The chief political result of the same combination is the necessity for a power structure not subject to audit and invested with a mythical legitimacy. Of all the elements making up these syncretic production relations, those of a precapitalist character exert the strongest influence on the political power, since that character is nothing other than the absorption of such production relations by that power. That is why precapitalism is a coparticipant in the economy but dominant in politics.

After having rejected objective necessity *qua* private ownership, the regime lets itself be swamped by objective necessity *qua* property vacuum coupled with the separation between workers and management. Thus the society escapes the dominion of one kind of necessity only to come under that of another—one that the regime takes to be the dominion of freedom, simply because it was the former that laid its foundations.

Unlimited power is only the illusion generated by conditions that the regime persists in believing it has created all by itself, without realizing that it has become the object of those conditions. Unlimited power is a basic form of the false consciousness characteristic of Stalinist society.

The conversion of production relations into relations of force made possible the effective abolishment of private ownership of the means of production. Once stabilized and reproduced, that same conversion transformed a revolutionary society into one based on command—a specifically feudal-type structure.

While denying the workers access to ownership, the Stalinist dispensation offers them, in exchange, its effective protection against the restoration of capitalist private ownership, and against imperialist domination. In this way the identity of the command regime is fully revealed, since protection is an essentially feudal justification for relations of dependence. Every command regime claims to be a protective regime. In the case of Stalinism, protection against capitalist economic constraint is assured by the Stalinist extra-economic coercion.

Stalinism is a society based on command, without being a feudal society. Its regression toward the feudal model is considerable but incomplete. It is not characterized by the specifically feudal forms of ownership and appropriation; the means of production are in effect expropriated from the producers; the labor power is economically compelled to find a market for itself; the means of production and the technical organization of work have an industrial character which becomes dominant; the power structure rules out any territorial or other type of dispersion, remaining strictly centralized on the national level; etc. (The present writer's emphasis on the concept of a command regime is intended to bring out both the similarities and the distinctions between Stalinism and feudalism.) The effective negation of capitalism achieved thanks to this regression is not transformed into an effective affirmation of socialism.

Stalinism's penchant for the feudal model is not only

something incomplete: it is coupled with a kind of economic mechanics that is specifically monopolistic. The specific actions of monopolies consist in breaking the rules of the capitalist economy by imposing nonequivalent exchanges. Stalinism transfers this monopolist principle from one economic sector to the entire national economy, and primarily to a domain usually inaccessible to capitalist monopolies: the purchase of labor power. In combining the command economy with monopolistic methods, Stalinism makes nonequivalent exchange the foundation of the production relations peculiar to it.

One important result of the alliance between monopoly and the command system is the Stalinist price-fixing system. Under capitalism, the monopolies get around the tendentious economic law according to which price should be the measure of value. In so doing, they are actually challenging the economic system that has engendered them: they place themselves outside of it, while pretending to remain within it. Objectively, the monopolies harm capitalism in this way, although their aim is not to weaken it but merely to increase their profits. This objective anticapitalist element, inherent in the practices of the monopolists, is taken over by Stalinism with the double aim of financing industrialization and making the abolishment of capitalism irreversible.

Thus the Stalinist type of anticapitalism is at once precapitalist and monopolist in character. As a result, the property vacuum is converted by Stalinism into free access to all forms of anticapitalism except the one with which it claims kinship.

The privilege of controlling a branch of the economy unbeknownst to the latter, which is clandestine in the case of monopolies, is transformed by the command system into a right that is juridically ratified and hence valid for the entire national economy. The main difference, however, between the practice of the monopolies and that of Stalinism lies not in its radius of action, its legality, or its aim, but in its mechanism. Monopolies make for deterioration of the relation between price and value, while Stalinism makes for deterioration of value itself. It does so via its special control of labor power, by imposing a division of labor largely indifferent to viable demand. The result is that a great part of social labor is, in economic terms, socially unnecessary; and work that is socially unnecessary does not produce value. The systematic expenditure of unnecessary salaried labor makes objectively necessary the extra-economic determination of its value, and hence of its price and the price of its product. The monopolistic practices of Stalinism are not only ratified by law, they are demanded by the economy.

The geometric point where the fusion between monopoly and the command system takes place is the power structure: the arbitrary authority tends to become a monopoly of power which behaves like an economic monopoly. By virtue of its broad jurisdiction, the arbitrary authority, based on monopoly, acquires a degree of power that cannot be compared either to the feudal dispensation or to the capitalist monopolies. In a very general way, the function of noneconomic prices consists in disguising commands in the clothing of value. Manipulated from the outside, the price mechanism is transformed into a tool of the regime. Imperious decisions take on the appearance of equivalent exchanges. The arbitrary authority resorts to a debasement of value only to take better advantage of it. From its point of view, these prices do not so much have the function of dissimulation as that of amplification. With the help of sham prices, extra-economic coercion is strengthened by the energy of economic compulsion. The regime's subjective decisions are manifested as objective behaviors on the part of the workers. In this context, to buy and sell at noneconomic prices is to make operative the decisions of the arbitrary authority. Coercive decision making only absorbs, assimilates, and multiplies the compulsory power of prices. Put into practice on a basis that represents their negation, prices, although alienated from their essence, lend to that negative basis their organizing capacity. Needless to say, this osmosis between economic compulsion and extra-economic coercion confers upon the arbitrary authority an insurmountable ambiguity. The latter represents the source of the excessive power accruing to that authority.

Although alienated from their original content, value, noneconomic prices keep intact their prohibitive function. Just as in a market economy, it is always they which separate human needs from their objects. This functional continuity shows how capable prices are of remaining indifferent to their content. Moreover, in using them in this way, the regime adds to its monopoly on recourse to violence, a monopoly on the legal perturbation of economic rules that the workers must respect in the most inflexible way.

But Stalinism is something more than a combination of the feudal command system with monopolistic practices: its syncretic economy also includes methods peculiar to the primitive accumulation of capital. The realization of a noncapitalist primitive accumulation was a vital necessity that history made incumbent upon the premature socialist society. Stalinism is not the creator of that necessity but a definite way of responding to it.

History knows no industrialization that was not nourished by a process of primitive accumulation. Itself descended from that process on the national level, imperialism became its chief obstacle on the international plane. Stalinism is the historical proof of the fact that that obstacle can be overcome thanks to the Leninist revolution, which created the possibility of an anticapitalist industrialization. Stalinism is the transformation of that possibility into a reality. Its feat of industrialization could only have begun with the identification and use of the sources of accumulation.

Right on the heels of its victory, the anticapitalist anticipatory revolution was faced with the overtly capitalist task of unleashing and making full use of the primitive accumulation or its equivalent—something indispensable to industrialization. This task was not created by Stalinism; it was merely taken on by the latter.

For Marx, "so-called primitive accumulation is (therefore) nothing other than the historical process of separation between the producers and the means of production." Socialism is called upon to abolish that separation. Premature socialism cannot avoid it; Stalinism uses it as a foundation.

In its capitalist version, this separation is perfectly clear. It comprises, on the one hand, the expropriation of the means of production from the producers and, on the other, the accumulation of those same means in the hands of the new proprietors; *ergo*, their transformation into capital. Although just as clear for practical purposes, this separation under Stalinism is economically vague and juridically nonvalidated. In this case, the dispossession of the producers is added to that of the capitalists. The economically confused state of affairs results from the fact that this generalized dispossession is not followed by any effective transfer of ownership. The property vacuum comes into being; and the separation between producers and means of production, rather than disappearing, merely changes its form. Ratified by capitalist law, this separation is challenged by Stalinist law. Being legal under capitalism, the condition of the producers lends itself to a kind of regulation that is above all economic. Being illegal under Stalinism, that condition demands a kind of regulation that is above all extra-economic and hence coercive.

Just as under capitalism, the Stalinist primitive accumulation bases the separation between producers and means of production on a depreciation of the value of labor power and an organization of the labor process that is coercive to the point of brutality. These methods, transient under capitalism, have been rendered irreversible by Stalinism. They are not secondary but essential to production relations in a command economy. Stalinism is an anticapitalist mode of production based on the perpetuation of capital's methods of primitive accumulation. The same command system that makes industrialization possible, makes the emancipation of the producers impossible.

The primitive accumulation of capital was determined by

the historical process whereby capital became the dominant form of proprietorship; and its duration was equal to the lifetime of that process. Anticapitalist primitive accumulation is determined by the command structure of the Stalinist economy; and its duration will be equal to the lifetime of that structure.

In its capitalist version, primitive accumulation had a univocal economic legitimacy: the underdeveloped state of the productive forces. In its Stalinist version, it has a bivalent legitimacy: on the one hand, the underdeveloped state of the productive forces; on the other, the structures erected to eliminate that underdevelopment. This bivalent legitimacy contains the seeds of its possible separation into two distinct legitimacies. Once industrialization has taken off, capitalism can gradually abandon the methods of primitive accumulation. But in the same situation, Stalinism cannot abandon its structure. Under Stalinism the methods of primitive accumulation do not disappear as industrialization progresses but rather persist by virtue of the command structure—something for which they are inalienable.

Thus Stalinism turns out to be a mode of production that prolongs the process of primitive accumulation after the latter's economic legitimacy has died out. In this sense, Stalinism and primitive accumulation are inseparable. In this light, Stalinism can be viewed as a mode of production that converts the transient methods of capitalist primitive accumulation into the unvarying laws of an anticapitalist command economy—laws that function indefinitely, quite independently of the productive forces. In the long run, this economy of anticapitalist primitive accumulation destroys, with its own feats of industrialization, any economic legitimacy for its perpetuation.

It is precisely this loss of legitimacy which indicates the transformation of Stalinism into neo-Stalinism. Under Stalinism it is the necessity for primitive accumulation which imposes a definite structure on society. Under neo-Stalinism it is that consolidated structure which imposes primitive accumulation. In perpetuating the methods of primitive accumulation despite the progress made, the arbitrary authority no longer submits to necessity: it replaces the latter. Stalinism, characterized by obedience to necessity, becomes neo-Stalinism, characterized by an ignorance of necessity. The first goal of Stalinism was to prevent the restoration of capitalist private ownership; the first goal of neo-Stalinism is to prevent the restoration of social property. The significance of the property vacuum becomes its own opposite. Stalinism is a nonsocialist social order of progressive complexion. Neo-Stalinism is a nonsocialist social order of regressive complexion.

Stalinism does not pass from one stage to another by virtue of its inner evolution but by virtue of its inertia. Stalinism becomes neo-Stalinism owing to its capacity to change its ambiance, coupled with its incapacity to change itself.

Without being the inevitable result of premature socialism, Stalinism is its real continuer—the most durable and the most widespread one. It does not make premature socialism move ahead toward its maturity, but it does preserve its essential traits—its anticapitalism and its anti-imperialism. These two traits have been very much questioned by numerous critics of contemporary Stalinism, who define it as State capitalism or neo-imperialism. No doubt neo-Stalinism comprises elements of monopolistic State capitalism and of imperialism. But it also includes elements—and these are even more potent—of precapitalism and postcapitalism. It is only by resisting the temptations offered by one-to-one analogies and by assuming the aforementioned basic syncretism, that theory can move ahead toward an understanding of this mode of production in all its baffling detail.

THESES

I. THE SYNCRETIC SOCIETY

1. One cannot isolate the evolution of premature socialism from the conditions of its birth. Those conditions took shape around the international collision between underdevelopment and imperialism; or, to put it another way, around the obstruction of industrialization in the imperialist era.

2. The historical evidence presents three different responses to the obstacles that imperialism set up in the way of industrialization:

a. Resignation, which meant the reproduction of underdevelopment in various forms;

b. Opposing imperialism by forming new imperialisms. Germany, Japan, and Italy are countries to be classed not as underdeveloped but as belated industrializers. Ultimately, this response manifested itself in world wars which the neo-imperialists lost militarily but won economically: their industrialization has been accomplished.

c. The Leninist revolution, which by combining the anti-imperialist and anticapitalist traits became a dual-purpose historical instrument. Being possessed of this characteristic, the Leninist revolution, contrary to the militarist solution, did not oppose imperialism by imitating it but rather by negating its very essence; viz., the very principle of the private ownership of the means of production.

3. Imperialist war and Leninist revolution have both shown themselves to be effective ways of industrializing. Both of these ways are political, which proves that the extra-economic oppression put to use by imperialism cannot be destroyed by means that are solely economic. But while the wars have resulted in nothing more than the territorial extension of the imperialist model, the Leninist revolution, despite its grievous subsequent distortions, continues to be material proof that a feasible alternative to the imperialist organization of the world does exist. (Of course this is true only provided that the aforementioned distortions are corrected in time for the nations of Leninist stock to be able to avoid passing from the negation of imperialism to its imitation.)

4. The underdeveloped countries, dominated by a capitalism which is itself underdeveloped, have little chance of avoiding their subordination to imperialism, and of industrializing. For it is thanks to the same imperialism they challenge on the political plane, that their national capitalism is, in the short run, able to expand its profits.

5. The economic convergence between national capitalism and foreign imperialism, especially at the turn of the century, represented an objective fact largely independent of political relations. Such being the case, the Leninist strategy, whose chief aim was to unite the anti-imperialist revolution with the anti-capitalist one, was a perfectly logical (if not the only) alternative to the perpetuation of underdevelopment.

6. History has since proven that the foundations of this strategy were sound. It was a strategy that made possible the lasting elimination of foreign imperialist domination and of domestic capitalist domination; and it also made accelerated industrialization possible. What it did not make possible, however, was an effective transition to a socialist organization of society.

7. Premature socialism thus showed itself to be an effective

46

way of organizing industrialization in the imperialist era. Imperialism's opposition to all industrialization but its own is the first source of the present contradiction between socialism and industrialization.

8. This means that anti-imperialist and anticapitalist industrialization is not "socialist industrialization" (an ideological formula which is a contradiction in terms). The reduction of socialism to anti-imperialist and anticapitalist industrialization is the fundamental ideological illusion of premature socialism, whose basic syncretism it expresses.

9. From a functional point of view, the deepest roots of this syncretism are located precisely in the ability to combine economic affirmation, as expressed in industrialization, with social affirmation, as expressed in socialism.

10. The forced implantation of a revolutionary class structure in an underdeveloped economy presupposes the forced preservation of the way in which those classes are articulated. But it is precisely the lack of a natural articulation which perpetuates their incompatibility, and hence the syncretism of the whole.

11. This disarticulation stems from the abolishment of private ownership of the underdeveloped means of production, which demanded such ownership. The social character of those means of production thus contradicts their technological character. Challenged by the economic reality, the social structure assumes an ideological legitimacy.

12. Premature socialism combines a market economy with a social structure that excludes the private ownership of the means of production as manifested in the propertied classes.

The social structure prevents the market economy from achieving its functional goal, which is to establish private ownership. The market economy prevents the class structure from taking on an economic legitimacy consisting in the true socialization of the means of production.

Thus the syncretism of premature socialism manifests itself most plainly in the incompatibility between its social and its economic organization.

13. The social organization aspires toward dominion over the economy, but succeeds only in hampering the latter's action.

14. The social organization aspires toward independence from the economy, but succeeds only in becoming separate from it.

15. Separation is an illusory form of independence, since such independence of the social structure from the economy implies equal independence of the economy from the social structure.

16. The combination of these separate elements, going against the imperative of history, is based on the imperative of organized will as expressed in the power structure.

17. The two social elements are incompatible. It is the function of the regime (power structure) to make their articulation at once possible, enduring, and (especially) effective with respect to the dynamics of industrialization.

18. Social syncretism therefore includes a third element: an immense power structure, autonomously organized, which reproduces the incompatibility and the coexistence of the other two elements.

19. In this case, then, we are dealing not with a *system* of premature socialism but with a nonsystemic conglomerate, each real system of which constitutes one of those elements. What binds this artificial construction together could hardly be other than coercive force.

20. Premature socialism represents a nonsystem whose goal is to become a system by harmonizing the economic organization with the social order (and not the other way around). It follows, in such a case, that the routine use of the tools of systems analysis has heuristic value only if that analysis includes in its premises the nonsystemic nature of the object of study.

21. This means that one can treat the three elements—the economy, the class structure, and the power structure—as so many autonomous systems, but not as components of a single system at the level of the society as a whole; and that one can study the way in which those elements are articulated in order

to discern not only the functional aspects but (especially) the dysfunctional consequences of that articulation.

Proprietorship

22. The syncretism of the society as a whole reappears in specific forms at the economic level. So long as the absence of propertied classes, on the one hand, and the presence of a regime regulating all social activity, on the other hand, represent undeniable realities, the economy cannot avoid the repercussions of this environment. The most general function of this structural syncretism is to assure the effectiveness of capitalist mechanisms at the level of the production-distribution cycle and, at the same time, their total replacement by the decisions of the regime at the level of appropriation and investments. To put it differently, the role of syncretism, as applied to the economy, is to assure simultaneously the functioning and malfunctioning of the capitalist economic mechanisms needed for industrialization.

23. The syncretism of the economy consists essentially in the undefinable nature of proprietorship.

24. The alternative that this regime offers to the absence of the private ownership of the means of production, is another absence: that of the social ownership of those same means.

25. In its turn, the regime has a monopoly not on the ownership of those means but on the control of that ownership.

26. Thus to power based on property, which characterizes capitalism, premature socialism opposes the monopolistic control of property based on power.

27. The underdevelopment of the productive forces does not exclude their expropriation from private owners, but it does prevent their effective appropriation by the producers. The prematurity of the regime consists precisely in its determination to socialize underdevelopment. The property vacuum is the result of effective expropriation coupled with an inoperative socialization.

The premature socialization of the underdeveloped means of production brackets the society between the political rejection of private ownership and the economic impossibility of social ownership. It is this cleavage which appears as a vacuum of ownership of the means of production.

It is this recourse to the economic expedient of a property vacuum which makes necessary the syncretism of the mode of production. And it is the syncretism of the mode of production which makes possible the property vacuum peculiar to anticapitalist industrialization.

28. Defined in relation to this mode of proprietorship, premature socialism represents a social order which is not so much socialist as anticapitalist.

29. This transitional attribute takes on the dimensions of an era. Premature socialism is the historical stabilization of that moment, ephemeral by nature, when the object of negation is equally intolerable and indispensable to the subject. It is this indefinable identity which engenders the syncretism of premature socialism.

Labor Power

30. Before taking on a redistributive [*justitiaire*] function, premature socialism has an industrializing function imposed on it by the actual state of the productive forces. The fundamental law of industrialization is the same as that of capitalism: labor power must be transformed into a saleable commodity.

31. At this point, the incompatibility between the social order and the economic organization takes on a paradoxical form: labor power *must* be sold, but it *cannot* be bought. The industrializing economy rapidly expands the proletariat—the class of those who sell labor power—while the social structure prevents the formation of an opposing class of buyers for that same labor power—the owners of the means of production.

32. Under premature socialism, the role of that abolished

class is assumed by the State; viz., by the revolutionary regime. Premature socialism eliminates the capitalist incarnation of return realized from the purchase of labor power, but not the reality of that return.

33. Industrialization feeds on accumulation. With low labor productivity, the chief source of accumulation is not so much the increasing surplus product as the reduction in the amount of necessary labor.

34. In order to effect that reduction, the regime systematically assigns to labor power a price lower than its historically determined value.

35. Thus anticapitalist industrialization requires not only the preservation of the commodity nature of labor power but the fraudulent manipulation of its value by means of a dictated price.

36. At the level of economic interests—viz., immediate ones —this servitude sets the working-class regime in opposition to that class itself. In this way, the regime's legitimacy is transferred from the economic to the ideological sphere.

37. Ideology projected into the future becomes the systematic negation of the real in favor of the potential. The regime itself begins to serve the potential class to the detriment of the actual class.

38. Supplementary appropriation is a burden on consumption. Underconsumption as a strategy of accumulation is added to underconsumption as a consequence of underdevelopment.

39. This strategy of accumulation is most harsh as applied to agricultural production. The prices fixed for the products of this sector have no relation to the latter's value. This form of the circulation of goods comes close to confiscation, and preserves merely the appearance of economic exchange.

40. The temptation offered by confiscation, which in its outright form was abandoned along with War Communism, survived for more than three decades in this illusory form. It, more than anything else, nourished the accumulation of capital.

41. The noneconomic prices fixed for agricultural products

signify the devaluation, without any yardstick, of labor power in agriculture.

42. In the long run, the greater the gap between the real and the recognized value of labor power, the more labor productivity diminishes.

43. This is the chief reason why, under premature socialism, the general productivity of labor is not competitive with that under advanced capitalism, even when the equipment is identical. It also explains why, within that low level, the productivity of agricultural labor is noticeably lower than that of industrial labor.

44. Thus industrialization, which aims at raising labor productivity, is itself achieved by means which inhibit the development of labor productivity.

45. Under premature socialism, by contrast with precapitalist formations, the different modes of production do not coexist in parallel planes but are articulated in one single economic process. The syncretism of the economy, therefore, does not consist in the plurality of those modes of production but in the heterogeneous nature of the single functioning mode of production.

46. This internalized syncretism is both the product and the producer of the property vacuum. The economic coherence of the process is coupled with its social incoherence. The three elements—social structure, economic mechanisms, and political power—exert incompatible influences in each phase of the process. This general confusion, however, does not exclude a certain functional division: any given phase is dominated by only one element.

47. Thus:

a. The regime, being of precapitalist complexion, affects chiefly the allocation of production tasks and the distribution of the social product. It is this element which determines the status of labor power;

b. The capitalist mechanisms affect mainly the articulation

between production and consumption. It is owing to these mechanisms that labor power preserves its commodity character, and that surplus accumulation based on underconsumption thus becomes possible. The plan itself is drawn up in the language of the market. So it is that labor power is subjected to a double compulsion: an extra-economic one imposed by the regime, and an economic one imposed by the capitalist mechanisms. The precapitalist-type regime and the capitalist mechanisms operate toward the same goal: accelerated industrialization;

c. The new class structure exerts a decisive influence in the phase of the appropriation of the social product. It is this element which prevents private appropriation of the latter. Thus the regime makes it possible to eliminate traditional parasitic consumption, and in so doing prepares the way for the transformation of the social product into social accumulation.

48. The difficulty lies not only in defining this mode of production but in determining whether the very concept of mode of production is applicable here. And yet intellectual constructs must yield to the facts, which prove that this syncretic mode of production exists from the moment when it succeeds in fulfilling its two incompatible functions: industrialization on the one hand, and reproduction of the absence of capitalist private ownership on the other. On the basis of these functional accomplishments, it may be possible to regard this mode of production as one peculiar to anticapitalist industrialization.

49. It is the syncretism of the economic process which prevents any systemic unity on the structural level, while at the same time permitting systemic performance of a negative kind on the functional level; viz., the reproduction of the property vacuum. It is no doubt the interacting pressure between the precapitalist-type regime, the capitalist economic mechanisms, and the socialist class structure which prohibits scarcity from following its spontaneous tendency to reconvert to private ownership of the means of production.

Class

50. Consequently, the different production relations, in their turn, coexist not only at the level of society as a whole but also at the level of the different processes. It is this vertical diffusion of a generalizing tendency which transforms precapitalist heterogeneousness into anticapitalist syncretism.

51. Thus, for example, the production relations characterizing the social and economic conditions of the working class combine the following elements:

a. socialist determinations consisting in: the absence of an opposing class, of the kind of exploitation that yields private profit, and of unemployment; considerable access to education, housing, social security, and retirement benefits; incomparable promotion opportunities; and effective priority access to leadership positions;

b. capitalist determinations consisting in: the economic necessity of selling one's labor power; participation in the appropriation of the social product in the form of a wage; commercial consumption; separation from the means of production and the product; inaccessibility to decision making; subjection in the area of self-reproduction as labor power;

c. determinations of a precapitalist, feudal complexion consisting in fixing the productive tasks and the opportunities for consumption by means of coercive decisions; an authoritarian, nonnegotiable, and unfavorable determination of the value of labor power; a labor productivity generally below the normal performance of the equipment utilized (something typical of any allocative economy and any coercive organization of labor); the absence of operative class organizations; political apathy; social isolation; personal dependence; the pursuit of social advancement not by means of revolutionary class action against the system but through personal loyalty to immediate superiors, and hence to the system; and the substitution of regressive, explosive discontinuity in class struggles for daily continuity and the integration of such struggles.

From this it follows that under premature socialism the course taken by differentiation deviates from Parsons' model. Here it is not manifested in the multiplication of functionally defined elements but in a functional syncretism—hence the incoherence within each element.

The Regime

52. Social syncretism is naturally also the syncretism of the power structure that it incarnates. The general function of that power structure (the regime) is manifold. It defends the social structure against the economy, the economy against the social structure, and itself against both of these. It is at once the protector and the disturber of both the social structure and the economy.

53. This regime is socialist, because in achieving anti-imperialist and anticapitalist industrialization it erects a real and necessary premise for socialism in underdeveloped countries.

54. But the direct conversion of the social product into social accumulation, which the new class structure makes possible, is badly distorted by the underdevelopment of the productive forces. In aiming to reconcile the two terms, the regime contributes its own distortion.

55. To the extent that it assumes this role, the regime also takes on a markedly capitalist complexion.

56. On the other hand, this regime confers upon itself a charismatic and repressive legitimacy. It couples economic compulsion with extra-economic coercion so as to assign both the productive tasks and a price of labor power which is lower than its real value. To this end it prohibits the producers from using any regular means of defense. All of the foregoing are deeply ingrained traits of a specifically feudal character.

57. Given the actual underdevelopment of this society, its historical origin, and the specific potential of the coercive model of feudalism, it is the uncontrolled propensity toward

that model which confers upon the premature socialist regime its predominant character.

58. The syncretism of the regime is manifested above all in the incongruence of the functions it assumes. The exercise of those functions undergoes evident modification in the course of time. But the modification in the exercise of its functions is coupled with the rigidity of its structure. And it is that structure, rather discrete, which quite independently of its functional aspects, confers upon the regime its true identity, which is preponderantly feudal.

59. Its syncretism allows the regime to have simultaneous access to all the forms of coercion elaborated in the course of history.

The Dynamics

60. The structural-functional syncretism is repeated in the long-range dynamics of each fundamental element. At first glance a clear incongruence is discernible: on the one hand the dynamism of the economy, on the other the immobilism of the social structure and the regime. These two make each other possible.

61. The same syncretism is concealed behind the apparently univocal nature of these various dynamics. On the historical scale, each of these types of movement lacks unity.

62. Thus the dynamism of the economy combines the accelerated development of the productive forces with the very slow development of consumption, and with the stability of the fundamental mechanisms: the commodity character of labor power, the property vacuum, the way centralized planning combines recourse to the market with opposition to it, and the coercive pricing policy.

63. The immobilism of the social structure is coupled with the frenetic mobility of individuals. The basic direction of this mobility is the shift from agriculture to industry—the prole-

tarianization of the peasant masses manifested as urbanization. The majority constituted by the peasantry is rapidly reduced in favor of the proletariat, the intelligentsia, and the bureaucracy. The classes remain the same, but their relations change.

64. Finally, the immobilism of the regime is tied in with its essential structure: centralization, exemption from audit, etc. Industrial progress makes this sytem of political control more and more decrepit. That is why the immobilism of the power structure is coupled with the mobility of the individuals who embody it, and with the way in which they try to utilize it.

65. Thus what we have here is not a mere regressive tendency but a syncretism which, in the last analysis, defines the same historical movement unleashed by premature socialism. This movement is at once revolutionary and regressive. The most comfortable assumption—but not necessarily the most relevant one—is that, projected in opposite directions, the movement approaches zero. But the mere thought of the industrial dynamics suffices to cast doubt on that assumption.

66. It would seem more correct to say that, left to the mercy of spontaneity—and hence of accidents—either of these two movements could, at a given moment, prevail over the other. Thus in order to improve the odds for the progressive direction, premature socialism should replace spontaneity with strategy and ideology with theory.

Values

67. The general syncretism of this society is inevitably expressed in the incongruence of the value systems governing its existence.

68. The model for the syncretism of values is provided by the most vital activity: production. The economic organization of the productive process is coupled with the noneconomic valuation of its results. This is the case for those types of production considered useful despite their being economically unprof-

itable—the so-called planned losses—owing to which profitability is sacrificed to industrialization. Or, more generally, it is the case for the coercive price of labor power.

69. This does not mean that the regime only opposes social rationality to economic rationality. Rather, it opposes its own rationality to both of them.

70. As the defender of social rationality, the regime takes on a heavily socialist coloring; as the initiator of economic development, a capitalist one; and as an autonomous element subject to its own rationality, a feudal one.

71. All coherent and operational value systems are at once rational in themselves and irrational with respect to other, hence incompatible systems.

72. This means that one and the same action takes on incompatible values if its effect is judged according to value systems which are themselves incompatible.

73. The axiological syncretism of premature socialism, which tries to combine three distinct rationalities—those of the social structure, the economy, and the political structure—culminates in irrationality at the level of the whole assemblage.

74. The mechanism whereby the political regime fulfills its function as a dispenser of irrationality consists in imposing on one element the rationality of another. At what time, in what proportion, to what extent, and by virtue of what motivations it does this to the advantage or disadvantage of one element or another—these are the parameters of an autonomous rationality: that of the regime.

75. Without a basic theory which would allow for a well worked-out strategy, the rationality of the political regime tends naturally to manifest itself as irrationality. This is why its self-assigned privilege of imposing meta-economic reasons on the economic rationality, has since 1960 been the favorite target of reformers.

76. From this angle of vision, the spirit of the economic reforms attempted in the premature socialist countries could be translated into the following propositions:

1. It does not suffice for a given rationality that it be meta-economic in order for it to be, at the same time, preferable to an economic rationality;

2. At least under the given circumstances, the autonomous rationality of the regime, which tends toward arbitrary incoherence, is not preferable to the rationality of the economy, which tends toward a coherence regulated in an impersonal fashion.

77. Axiological syncretism confers a connotative attribute upon every human action.

78. This means that:

1. Every action can become the object of judgments that are in the same degree, different from one another and legitimate;

2. This independence between action and judgment necessitates a judicial authority which is itself exempt from all judgment, hence exempt from audit, and infallible;

3. The same axiological confusion creates the contrary possibility: every human action could be mistaken. The fact that actions and judgment are independent of each other leads to the unprecedented socialization of guilt—an indispensable corollary of the centralization of infallibility.

79. Under these conditions, feedback becomes not merely useless but impossible. The fact that each of the signs has many significations makes them illegible.

80. The elimination of feedback represents the triumph of grand strategy over tactics—of unconditioned teleology over conditioning.

81. This topsy-turvy state of affairs finds expression in the tremendous latitude of the regime as manager. It judges its economic management in social terms. This transfer of values from one domain to another makes it possible for the growth of unprofitable (hence economically intolerable) production—which, however, is useful to industrialization, and hence socially positive—to reproduce itself indefinitely, with a surprising indifference toward its true specificity.

Theory

82. All social theory is the anticipation of a becoming which represents the transformation of the possible into the real. All social practice inspired by an anticipatory theory is therefore teleological—action subordinated to a predetermined end.

83. As theory degenerates into ideology, the teleology is reversed. No longer are actions subordinate to the end. On the contrary, it is the end which is subordinated to the actions. Or, to put it differently, the end has a tendency to dissolve in actions. The transformation of the actual is confined to its reproduction.

84. The reproduction of the actual seeks legitimacy in its ideological representation.

85. Since practice not buttressed by theory is impotent, the end is shifted to the sphere of ideology.

86. Once implanted in ideology, the end is no longer the subject of transformation, but its object. Instead, now, of inspiring the conversion of the possible into the actual, it inspires its own involution: from strategic opposition to a pragmatic submission to necessity.

Convergence

87. The syncretic bent of premature socialism has other causes as well. Unlike the formations that preceded it, capitalism is a mode of production that devours all the others: the mode of production and the social formation merge. Capitalism cannot exist without this exclusivist tendency. To oppose it with a contrary tendency is either to prevent capitalism from existing, or to revive it. The syncretism of premature socialism therefore represents a specific way of negating capitalism by negating the systemic homogeneousness which is its *sine qua non.*

88. The implication here is that any way of negating capi-

talism is better than capitalism itself. In this case a negation of regressive character would be a useful subsidiary to the revolutionary negation.

89. The factual syncretism of premature socialism discloses, at one and the same time, the merits and the limitations of the theory which posits a convergence of the two systems: the merits, because that theory reflects the objective presence of economic mechanisms common to both capitalism and premature socialism; the limitations, because it overlooks the presence (likewise objective) of those precapitalist elements that advanced capitalism has long since abandoned.

90. Premature socialism stands in a relation of partial convergence not only toward capitalism but toward the underdeveloped countries; viz., toward precapitalism. And this capacity for incomplete resemblance to incompatible systems again proves that premature socialism is syncretic in nature.

Consequences

91. The syncretism of the social order, of its components, of its dynamics, of its axiological system, and of its own identity provokes on the part of the regime a frantic need for homogeneousness. That need is expressed on the one hand by the regime's tendency toward monolithism, and on the other by its bent toward personifying itself.

92. In other words, the worst excesses of this regime—its extreme centralization, its out-and-out monolithism, and its standardization of culture—are all aimed at compensating for the disruptive pressure of a generalized syncretism.

93. In the syncretic society, the hierarchy of structural elements remains flexible, while that of persons becomes extremely rigid.

94. The absence of any objective hierarchy—and hence of any dominant element—makes irrelevant any definition of this sociopolitical order, which does not admit to its own syncretism.

95. From a structuralist viewpoint, it is the unity based on the dominant element and its articulations which confers upon any complex system the attribute of structure.

96. Premature socialism deviates from this geometric image. It does not have a structural unity resulting from a coherent hierarchy of its elements. That is why, in its case, differentiation becomes destructuralization, and complexity becomes syncretism. What binds these incompatible elements together is the organized will, constantly reproduced, to articulate them. It is only in this light that the regime maintains a dominant position—a position that is not the result of social processes but, instead, is constantly being imposed upon them.

97. Since it is opposed to the actual tendencies, that will can be effective only by being coercive.

98. Premature socialism becomes less opaque when viewed from close up in terms of its structural-functional syncretism. This view enables us to recognize it as an incoherent rejection of capitalism.

99. Premature socialism achieves the incoherent rejection of capitalism by getting ahead of it, by assimilating it, and, at the same time, by regressing in relation to it.

100. The historical regression takes place primarily at the level of political power. It justifies itself by making possible the pursuit of anticapitalist and anti-imperialist industrialization.

101. To the extent that the regime assures industrialization, it exhausts the implied legitimacy of its regressive character.

102. In order to become effective, the regime has become an autonomous force. To the extent that—despite its loss of legitimacy and thanks to its already achieved autonomy—the regime persists in perserving its regressive character, premature socialism risks being reduced to a perverted socialism; i.e., to a rejection of capitalism that is as reactionary as it is effective.

II. THE ECONOMY

1. Viewed from without, the economy of premature socialism impresses one with its high degree of politicization and its effectiveness in industrialization. A sociological analysis of that economy is essential to an understanding of the socialist political system.

2. The basic trait of that economy is its ambiguity, which is ultimately due to the contradiction between the stage of development of the productive forces and their social character.

3. It is not this contradiction in itself which is peculiar to premature socialism, but the position of the opposing terms. In all previous societies, including capitalism, it was the technological development of the productive forces that took the lead, and their social character, concretized in forms of ownership and class structures, that lagged behind. It was the job of the political system to adapt the antiquated social character of the productive forces to their advanced stage of development.

The society of premature socialism was the first to have reversed this relation. Its political system endowed society with a class structure reflecting the effective elimination of the private ownership of the means of production. Thus the new social character of the productive forces did not adapt itself to, but for the most part ran ahead of, their actual stage of development. Here, in contrast to all previous history, the technological development lags behind the social.

[Page missing from the manuscript.—A.G.M.]

. . . egalitarian class formation, in the sense of a mutual absence of ownership of the means of production. From the angle of vision offered by this historical regularity, premature socialism can be interpreted as an inappropriate social organization of scarcity.

7. Under premature socialism the social ambiance of production is the socialist class structure, and the economic ambiance is scarcity. The goal of the regime—which is also the functional task of society—is to consolidate the social ambiance while destroying the economic ambiance.

8. Viewed in terms of its objective existence, premature socialism's most mobile element is its economy. That economy is supposed to reconcile the nonsocialist imperative of industrialization with the socialist class structure.

9. The new class structure expresses the abolishment of the private appropriation of the social product. This structure is therefore the social matrix of an egalitarian distribution plugged into an underdeveloped productive capacity. The social structure is nonfunctional because it represents an egalitarian distribution system deprived of its economic substance. This dysfunctionality is defined in relation to its socialist character. Premature socialism is thus a social order whose potential distribution capacity is very far in advance of its actual productive capacity.

10. The egalitarian class structure is a fascinating historical achievement. In fact, on its basis the society presumably has the function of building socialism. But underdevelopment is a ruthless historical legacy. Under its pressure, the society is compelled to take on the function of industrialization which, although an historic feat of great scope, is unrelated to the building of socialism.

11. Premature socialism is an attempt to respond to the condition of scarcity in a totally unprecedented manner. This novel way of organizing the distribution of scarcity proves that a growth in productivity is possible without society's being divided into proprietors and workers.

12. In the long run, the economy proves unresponsive to doctrine and even to ideology. It proves that emancipation from capitalist exploitation is not tantamount to emancipation from privation. Thus it demonstrates that exploitation is not the cause of scarcity but merely the preferred form in which it is manifested.

13. Scarcity is not a descriptive term for a state of poverty but rather an economic category. There is no scarcity apart from production. As an economic category, scarcity is an indicator of civilization; i.e., of that stage of development where reciprocal extermination is replaced by labor, so that nature is no longer the object of direct devastation but of devastating production.

14. Using these coordinates, I regard scarcity as that result of social production (but not of distribution) which keeps the workers' consumption at the level necessary for their reproduction as labor power. Although extremely relative, scarcity has remained a constant throughout history.

15. All the known models of premature socialism are marked by the same basic ambiguity. The latter is expressed in the discrepancy between the social structure and the industrializing function. (Exceptions: Czechoslovakia and the German Democratic Republic, where the discrepancy is much less marked but its effects are exacerbated by external pressures.)

16. Socialist construction makes the transition from the ideological sphere to the economic by way of industrialization. But the last-named is not socialist construction: it can be nothing more than its economic premise.

17. The two functions—socialist construction and presocialist industrialization—are at once incompatible and interconditioned. In this system, which is based on an historical asyn-

chronism whereby relations of sequence and causality are completely reversed, industrialization becomes the precondition for a probable socialist construction, which in turn becomes the ultimate aim of industrialization.

18. The most unquestionable achievement of premature socialism is the stabilized negation of the private ownership of the means of production. This negation does not actually put the ownership into the hands of the producers, but it represents the most solid premise history has so far erected for such a transfer.

19. Where is the ownership of the means of production under premature socialism?

The difficulty one has in answering this question stems from the uniqueness of that society. Previously, all forms of ownership had been crystallized into specific social structures that assured the dominant position of the class possessing the main means of production. But under premature socialism, the evolution of proprietorship does not reproduce this traditional process. In other words, there is no economic or juridical mechanism that assures ownership of the means of production by any one social class.

This remark also applies to theories of a "new class" defined according to criteria other than that of propietorship.

20. What with the new class relations, premature socialism creates an abeyance of ownership. Prohibited by the regime and attacked by restorative economic mechanisms, this elusive proprietorship leans more heavily than any other kind on juridical ratification.

21. The law can ratify ownership as ambiguity, thereby correctly expressing its ambiguous social situation. But this does not prevent the law, in so doing, from laying the foundations of an inevitable conflict between the two proprietary parties: the workers and the State. United by law, ownership is divided by politics. The unity of the subject and object of production cannot be based on their shared underdevelopment.

22. The law confers social ownership on the producers

without assuring their control of it. On the other hand, it assures such control by the State without conferring ownership on it. The control of property is separated from its possession, and the result is a property vacuum.

23. In this context, the socialist State assumes a double function: at one and the same time, it prevents the restoration of private, capitalist ownership, and the control of socialist property by the producers.

This paradoxical double function is a result of the basic ambiguity of the system.

25. The separation between juridical ownership and the control of ownership represents the embryo of a possible antinomy. Within this relation, the State is advantaged by the preeminence of the economic over the juridical. It is therefore the surrogate of a social ownership which the producers cannot control effectively because of the general underdevelopment. The State monopoly on the management of the economy thus expresses in a roundabout way the dominant underdevelopment. The State seems advantaged by a situation that it can neither ignore nor perpetuate indefinitely.

26. Under premature socialism the property vacuum in fact expresses a social leveling whose essence is the shared absence of proprietorship in the economic sense of the word. Being based on scarcity, this is already an invaluable achievement.

27. The essential ambiguity of the economy becomes transparent at the level of its mechanisms. Here value, money, salary, the surplus product, etc., get mixed up with planning, which converts the productive process into a political strategy.

28. The indifference of economic mechanisms toward individuals is the same under both capitalism and premature socialism. But capitalism as a system is, in its turn, indifferent toward that indifference, whereas premature socialism, because of its ambiguity, suffers a traumatized conscience from it.

29. The capitalist class structure is provided with economic mechanisms that are peculiar to it, and that make it functional. The socialist class structure has not managed to create specifi-

cally economic mechanisms suitable to itself. That is why relations between class structure and economic mechanisms represent an area of convergence under capitalism and one of divergence under premature socialism. In the latter case, it is the mechanisms of inequality which make the egalitarian structure inoperative. Under the pressure of scarcity, that structure coexists with elements that are its negation. The economic negates the social.

30. Premature socialism's recourse to the economic mechanisms of the system it negates does not at all imply capitulation. This is because, although premature socialism resorts to many mechanisms of the capitalist economy, it does not make use of the most important one: profit.

It is at this point that class structure comes into play. It does not govern economic activity, but it does regulate its results, since it replaces private appropriation of the social product with public appropriation.

This is not yet socialism, but it *is* a step toward a future socialism.

31. The survival of capitalist mechanisms in a noncapitalist society does not prove that they are perennial; it simply shows the limits of human intervention in the current of history. Thus that survival does not represent some evil destiny with which socialism is burdened but rather an inevitable condition of its premature version.

32. The economic mechanisms engendered by capitalist proprietorship tend spontaneously to reproduce that ownership, so that premature socialism can neither accept those mechanisms nor do without them. Their abolishment would make industrialization impossible, yet their functioning makes possible the restoration of capitalism. In reproducing this danger, premature socialism comes to suspect all economic mechanisms. And its intolerance toward spontaneity is displaced from the political sphere to economics.

33. All moral and political value judgments aside, these mechanisms fitted rationally into the capitalist system as a

whole. They were in their right place in an economy based on exploitation—one they served effectively. For those same mechanisms, however, premature socialism represents an artificial ambiance where that rationality is lost.

34. Society seems at times to have preserved those mechanisms chiefly in order to demonstrate their noxiousness. Their effect is so widespread, being founded on tradition and (especially) on the immediate interests of the vast majority, that it is impossible to subject it to thoroughgoing control. By escaping even partially from control, these economic mechanisms challenge the ideological image of a regime which aspires to being, and feels itself compelled to be, unlimited. Up to the present, history has known of no society which has not tampered with the workings of its economic mechanisms. The uniqueness of premature socialism consists in the systematic and deliberate character of such interventions. For it, interference with economic mechanisms becomes a political strategy.

35. The socialist State is not the owner of the means of production because:

1. such ownership is not recognized by the law (in a number of socialist countries);

2. there are no economic mechanisms allowing the State to utilize the fruits of social labor to the advantage of those representing the State.

What the State *does* possess as a possible attribute of ownership is the managerial function. In this respect there is an obvious resemblance between premature socialism and latter-day capitalism: both widen the separation between ownership and management. It is tempting to assume that this same effect is produced by the two opposite versions of the contradiction between the social character and the stage of technological development of the productive forces. On the other hand, this similarity as regards oppositeness also produces basically opposite effects.

36. In latter-day capitalism, this separation assures the reproduction of private ownership, whereas in premature social-

ism it prevents the restoration of such ownership by laying the groundwork for a possible effective socialization. Again, under capitalism management makes up a special class dependent upon the owners, whereas under socialism management constitutes a power structure upon which the owners in fact depend.

37. The producers base their ownership on:

1. its legal recognition, and

2. their ability to influence or determine the activity of management; viz., the State.

That ability, while insignificant on the operational level, is manifested on the level of basic orientations. It is expressed in such landmarks as the impossibility of restoring private ownership; the rapid progress of industrialization; the moderate yet very real increase in consumption; the promotion of workers to all echelons of leadership; progress in techniques of management (manipulation instead of repression, etc.).

The chief limitations of this ownership are:

1. inacessibility to direct management, and

2. the absence of economic mechanisms to assure the satisfaction of the workers' needs, outside of the economic compulsion that obliges them to sell their labor power and reproduce that process and that labor power.

38. The separation between ownership and management gives rise to the specifically socialist separation between leadership and production, and hence between the regime and the workers. The managerial authority "economizes" itself in the sense that it transfers methods of economic management to the sphere of political leadership.

Political rule over people is not replaced by an administration of things, as Saint-Simon and Engels believed. Under premature socialism, the administration of things becomes the administration of people. From the viewpoint of the regime, people and things are primarily perceived in terms of what they have in common; viz., as productive forces.

39. Property is not yet accumulated for the producers, but by them. It is their product, but not their possession. Their only

actual property is the same as under capitalism: their own labor power. Even if they are no longer exploited in the classic sense of the term, they are still deprived. The proletariat is transformed, but it does not wither away. All this can be boiled down to the statement that although one can totally modify the form of ownership, one can only partially modify the form of distribution. There is no more private appropriation of the fruits of social production; but that does not suffice to make the worker the owner of the fruits of his labor. Under the given conditions, scarcity remains the general object of distribution. That reality cannot be modified by transforming the system of ownership. At this stage the process of distribution is less dependent on its social framework than on its economic object.

40. The leadership may appear to be the proprietor of the national economy, but it does not become such. There is no economic mechanism that could make that possible. In order to be convinced of that, it suffices to consider only the most elementary facts. Item: the incomes of the leaders in no way depend on the economic results of their management, but they do depend on their political position. Item: the form of those incomes is always salary and never the private appropriation of surplus value. Item: there is no accumulation of fortunes, and certainly none in the form of means of production. Item: the prerogative of decision making is lost along with one's political position; hence it is only the expression of the latter. Item: membership in the ruling group cannot be passed on and cannot be inherited.

41. In doing away with profit, socialism has destroyed the economic mechanism which, under capitalism, measures in economic terms the degree to which management has adapted itself to existing conditions. In getting rid of that yardstick, socialist management has given itself a most unusual bent: that of remaining indifferent toward its own effects. It is this economically unresponsive management which serves as the basis for a generalized lack of audit as regards decision making.

42. The phenomenon thus revealed is one of an unprecedented interaction between decisions and results in the economic

sphere. The supreme law of capitalism keeps this relation within the limits of the immediate. There, adaptation to the effects of previous actions is a short-term process. The superiority of socialism consists in its patience. It can afford the apparent extravagance of ignoring the immediate effects of its economic decisions in favor of a general strategy. This is possible because of a limited autonomy with respect to production costs, cost price, profits, etc., based precisely on a specific separation between ownership and management. This indifference toward feedback goes beyond the economy and becomes a characteristic of the political system.

43. This freedom of decision making with regard to the immediate economic effects demands a considerable strengthening of the regime's authority and the official ideology. It is only by having recourse to excessive authoritarianism that the regime can stay in business despite the harmful effects of its decisions. Again, the ideology, by relating immediate effects to strategic goals, acts as a shock-absorber for the economic jolts caused by the regime's decisions. Thus it plays a directly economic role. It cannot endow the masses with a predictive consciousness; but it does gradually accustom them to thinking of the future—to an extent comparable only to the religious myth of the Last Judgment.

44. Under premature socialism, ownership is representative. This representativeness is not manifested mainly as a voting mechanism but as a substitution. The representative's function is to take the place of those he represents. Far from being an ideal model, representativeness shows the limits that the society imposes on the individual's self-assertion as a social being.

45. So long as the underdevelopment of the means of production obliges the State to personify social ownership, it is not within the State's power to do away with the separation between management and production. For underdevelopment, the true alternative to State management is not self-management but the restoration of capitalist-type private ownership.

46. Although born out of a disdain for the economy (see

Lenin and economism), the revolutionary regime keeps going by "economizing" itself. The rhythm of history takes vengeance on the rhythm of politics.

47. The ambiguity of the relations between political power and economic mechanisms is expressed in the ambiguous way those mechanisms are manipulated by the regime. The mistakes of the leaders offer only a conjectural explanation for the incoherence of that manipulation. In the long view, the latter is based on the objective incompatibility between that form of socialized ownership and those mechanisms.

48. To the extent that the regime succeeds in disturbing (and hence mitigating) the recurrent action of those hostile mechanisms, it creates, by the same token, the necessity for its decisions and the condition for their ineffectiveness.

The ambiguity of the effects reproduces the ambiguity of the system.

49. The legitimate tendency to keep a checkrein on the inherited mechanisms becomes an illegitimate tendency to use them as substitutes. Economic objectives are defined in political terms. Thus economic objectives are severed from the economy. To hinder the mechanisms means to prevent economic organisms from making a spontaneous adaptation to the motility of their context. Centralized decision making has to be more compelling than the economic imperative.

50. The basic cause of the confrontation between political power and economic mechanisms is their inequality. With scarcity predominant, the regime cannot renounce those mechanisms, which run counter to it; but the latter can get along very well—and even better than before—without the regime. If this observation is correct, it means simply that the action of those mechanisms is essentially autonomous with respect to the regime. What the latter prevents is not the action of those mechanisms but the natural effect of that action.

51. Hence there is a spontaneous incompatibility—one that is quite irreducible—between the capitalist economic mechanisms and the socialist regime.

The latter acts as if its capacity for intervening in the economy were unlimited. Now, a misjudgment of its real limits makes any strategy fragile, and poses the threat of its ending up in incoherence. By virtue of opposing the economic mechanisms in an incoherent manner, the regime gradually assumes their function: it becomes an economic mechanism.

52. The opposition between the socialist political regime and the capitalist economic mechanisms is a transfigured expression of the conflict between prematurely socialized ownership and the indispensable vestiges of private ownership. It shows the character of those inherited mechanisms to be at once indispensable and intolerable.

53. In keeping a rein on those mechanisms, the regime has the aim of protecting the new class structure. Under capitalism the class structure engenders the economic function of profits, which reproduces that structure. Under premature socialism the class structure does not engender the economic function of industrialization, which in turn does not reproduce that structure. Here, on the contrary, the nonsocialist economic function of industrialization threatens the socialist class structure.

The regime is the mediator between the two. So long as this dissonance is reproduced, the need for such mediation is also reproduced.

54. This situation takes on the temporal dimensions of an entire era. The mediating function thus has the respite in which to build tried-and-true mechanisms which, in time, are assembled into a system.

The system by means of which the dissonances between the social structure and the economic function are tempered, is the political system. The nature of the latter is much less the result of an autonomous strategy than of a spontaneous adaptation to inexorable conditions. At this level, strategy is only the language of necessity.

55. The primary function of politics is rejection. Politics rejects history. It believes it can impose its own laws on history

—which is true only up to a certain point. It does in fact inaugurate a new class structure; but it retraces its steps with regard to industrialization, which, far from representing any choice, is the functional acceptance of historical compulsion.

56. If the power structure were based on a sufficiently developed economy, it would not be compelled to transform itself into an economic mechanism. It would be able not only to destroy the mechanisms of the exploitative system but to build the mechanisms of a new system in which the economy, in its traditional role as the organizer of scarcity, would be perfected. There is only one way that premature socialism can move ahead in that direction. That way is to mature: to continue the industrialization of the economy and to replace the industrialization of theory by a valid theory of industrialization as a possible path toward socialism. This is the first condition for avoiding a situation in which the success of industrialization is manifested systematically as the crisis of socialism.

In the twenties, the triumphant revolution did not know what to do with its victory. Triumphant industrialization, owing to the skimpiness of theory that accompanies it, risks a return to that same point.

III. THE COMMAND ECONOMY

1. War Communism represented an attempt to bring the economy into step with the new social structure just set up by the revolution. The failure of War Communism confirmed Marx's thesis: production relations cannot develop independently of the existing productive forces. The confirmation of Marx's view by way of this failure poses the problem of the Marxist character of the Leninist revolution; or, more precisely, of the relation between Marxism and Leninism.

2. The next step, which amounted to a leap in the opposite direction, was the NEP; that is, making use of mechanisms peculiar to capitalism under the control of a fragile revolutionary regime whose immediate aim was to avoid, at one and the same time, the collapse of society and its own downfall.

3. The third attempt—one still in force, which represents the essence of Stalinism—involved the transformation of the regime into the sole dispenser of tasks and goods; something that the official ideology calls the building of socialism.

4. The sequence of the three solutions that have been tried expresses a structural syncretism and an attempt to assign the dominant position in turn to each of the fundamental elements:

to the social structure under War Communism, to the economy under the NEP, and to the power structure under the system of centralized allocation; i.e., the command system.

5. That same sequence also shows the linearity of the historical retreat. The power structure that imposed the revolution in spite of the general underdevelopment ends up by adapting itself to underdevelopment, the deliberate disregard of which enabled that structure to arise.

6. No sooner was the anticapitalist regime established, than it was compelled to recognize that under conditions of scarcity the mere abolishment of private property served only to reproduce that scarcity. Its true function, imposed by factual underdevelopment, was therefore not to build socialism immediately but to overcome scarcity as rapidly as possible; viz., to industialize. Its social aspirations suffered the great shock of the vast economic task imposed on it by history.

7. The historical contribution of that power structure consists in having achieved, under conditions of scarcity, both industrialization and the lasting abolishment of the private ownership of the means of production—two revolutionary reforms that are incompatible when they coincide historically.

8. The mechanisms of that achievement consists in banning economic competition of the capitalist type and replacing it with an arbitrary authority.

9. Capitalist competition, based on formal equality before the impersonal laws crystallized in the market, is a system for the distribution of inequality.

10. The general equality *vis-à-vis* the market is cancelled out by the inequality of the means making it possible to take advantage of those laws. The inequality of means is above all an inequality of property—the continuous hardening of discontinuous competition.

11. Although implanted somewhere outside of competition, property is at once its premise and its goal.

12. That explains why the abolishment of private property would be inoperative without the abolishment of capitalist com-

77

petition based on the laws of the market.

To be more exact: under premature socialism, command does not mean the elimination of the laws of competition but rather their systematic disruption, which consists in depriving them of their goals. This means that command is manifested not only in the disruption of those laws but in their operation as well: they function to the extent that the power structure tolerates them.

13. Actually, the model of a competitive economy is valid only as a methodological tool, since capitalism itself strives to destroy competition by means of monopolies.

14. The alternative to capitalist competition is socialist allocation.

15. Socialist allocation should represent the democratic organization of the distribution of resources.

16. Even in the advanced countries, socialism in its beginnings could hardly be anything more than a transition from the competitive organization of the economy to its allocative organization. Premature socialism should not, therefore, be blamed for trying to replace competition by allocation but for basing the latter on a combination of centralization and extra-economic compulsion. When mutilated, socialist allocation becomes arbitrary command.

16b. The first task of centralized allocation has a saliently restrictive character: it consists in preventing appropriation.

17. Given the historical conditions under which it took place and became stabilized, the conversion of the revolutionary regime into one based on command represents recourse to an essentially feudal mechanism: production and consumption are both regulated by extra-economic compulsion.

18. The command economy is engendered by the improvised application to scarcity of a system appropriate to conditions of abundance. This is the primary source of dogmatism.

19. The intolerance of this environment toward principles is merely an expression of the contradiction between socialism and underdevelopment.

20. The instrument intended to reconcile this contradiction is the feudal-type power structure mentioned above—one shaped by the factual underdevelopment but which believes itself not to have been so conditioned.

21. Command makes it not only possible but necessary that the power structure become autonomous with respect to the society.

22. This is because, in every arbitrary command system, the essential thing is the existence of an authority whose power —military, repressive, ideological—allows it to place itself above the rules.

Inconsistency in the rules (hence in the laws) is a condition inherent in arbitrary systems.

23. The general purpose of command is to solve by means of decision the same problems that competition solves spontaneously.

24. Under premature socialism, the basic tool of the command function is the plan.

25. The legitimacy of the command system is not so much economic as moral. Its morality lies in the effective rejection of private ownership of the means of production, without regard to the economic rationality of that rejection.

26. The arbitrary authority thus becomes the embodiment of social justice. That justice takes the form of an equal absence of freedom in the choice of both employment and consumption, the two of them being regulated by the central plan.

27. Hence justice remains within its historical bounds: its aspiration is to distribute coercion in a less inequitable manner.

28. Inevitably, the command system legitimizes itself through the trust that the dictator inspires. The form assumed by that trust—one as pure as it is rudimentary—is the attribute of infallibility. The charismatic leader is an economic imperative.

29. The charismatic leader is the alternative that premature socialism opposes to the market. Before coming to represent a deplorable abuse, he represents an economic mechanism whose function it is to make plausible—and hence bearable—a distri-

bution of scarcity which greatly favors production over consumption.

30. Coercion is not an alternative to the command system but rather its essence; because the true function of that system is the distribution of restrictions.

31. This explains why, in underdevelopment, the socialization of property begins with the socialization of coercion.

32. The system of commands is a totally nonsocialist form of the separation between production and appropriation. Socialism will begin with the abolishment of that separation.

33. The chief function assigned to the command system is to ban private appropriation, and hence profits. A secondary function resulting from the solution adopted—and thus from centralization—is to shield the process of accumulation against any social audit. It is this shielding function which makes possible the development of production based on the sacrifice of consumption.

34. These functions imply a triple negation: of profits, of social audit, and of consumption. That negation is placed in the service of a single affirmation: industrialization. Except in the last-named case, the command system is only the mirror image of a generalized prohibition, and thus of a generalized coercion.

35. Anti-imperialist and anticapitalist industrialization confronts the regime with two vital tasks: opposition to foreign domination, and the direct management of the economy.

36. But history does not limit itself to confronting premature socialism with these tasks: history offers it at the same time a long-tested operative model—that of the feudal system, which in a different context fulfilled similar functions.

37. The factual underdevelopment, the loss of theoretical perspective, the availability of this ready model, and the similarity of the tasks are the chief factors that engender the similarity of devices: the command economy, the hierarchical structures, personal dependence, and the preponderant role of the military and repressive apparatus which assures general application of extra-economic compulsion.

38. The specific weight of compulsion calls into question the definition of the historical trajectory actually described by premature socialism. In this light, premature socialism could be seen as marking the transition from a social order that transforms violence into regulated competition, to one that transforms regulated competition into unregulated violence.

39. The Marxism of Marx himself was a consonance between necessity, theory, and action. Leninism was an alliance of action and theory against necessity. Stalinism represents the sacrifice of theory, leading to a kind of action entirely subject to necessity and crystallized in the command system.

40. Leninism is the doctrine of the seizure of power by anti-imperialist and anticapitalist revolution, but not of the exploitation of that victory to the end of building socialism.

41. The essence of Stalinism consists in a confusion between anticapitalist industrialization and the building of socialism. What premature socialism loses because of that confusion is the understanding of its own identity and hence control over its development.

42. The resulting principle of Stalinism could be reduced to the postulate that any means useful to industrialization is good and can therefore be assimilated into socialism.

43. The imperative of industrialization presupposes a high rate of accumulation. Under conditions of imperialist hostility, the surplus product continues to be the main source of accumulation. In order to increase it, salary must represent a price of labor power that is lower than labor's real value.

44. For the producers, the wage—the specifically capitalist sale of their labor power—remains the basic form of appropriation.

45. The sale of labor power continues to be an economic reality; but its purchase, owing to the intrusion of the command regime, is a mere similitude. That bit of sham is expressed in the economically fictitious price of labor power.

46. Systematically to impose on labor power a price lower than its real value, implies the nonnegotiable fixing of salary.

Thus nonnegotiable salary becomes, regardless of its level, a resource allocated by command.

47. In order to be effective, the command system requires the suppression of economic dialogue; hence decisional monologue. This requirement is met by devitalizing all the political, social, and trade organizations that the workers set up for their defense in the course of that basic form of competition known as the class struggle.

48. The command system, which abolishes economic competition, also abolishes institutionalized class struggle.

49. Confronted with the class from which it emanates, the regime's command function is triply coercive: it secures more production as against less consumption by blocking any opposition by the producers, even in its potential stage.

50. Basing the increase of accumulation on a drastic reduction of consumption is a law characteristic of capitalist industrialization that premature socialism has not managed to escape.

51. Initially, at least, this antinomy tends to gravitate toward a separation between labor and needs. The perfect model of the irrelation between productive labor and the needs of the producers is forced labor.

52. This type of accumulation is conditioned by the regime's capacity to impose noneconomic prices. The model followed by premature socialism is that of the monopolies. Maximum profits and maximum accumulation both have recourse to the same mechanism, which consists in maintaining the pricing system in order to violate its rules. In addition to the filter of economic prices placed between the need and its object, a second filter is used: that of noneconomic, coercive prices which make the satisfaction of needs all the more difficult.

53. In the early stages of industrialization, the aim of production is its own expanded reproduction. So long as the development of production does not itself require an internal market, consumption—i.e., the economic rationality of needs—is a hindrance to accumulation, and hence to the rationality of industrialization.

54. Under any system of organizing scarcity, needs are forbidden from manifesting themselves otherwise than in the mystified form of economic interests. But the organization of scarcity characteristic of premature socialism tries to oppose this manifestation.

55. So long as use value assumes the prohibitive form of exchange value, human needs assume, in their turn, the mystified form of economic interests.

56. These two mutually disruptive conversions (of use value into exchange value, and of needs into interests) are characteristic of any unequal distribution of scarcity.

57. The general forms in which interest manifests itself are the private ownership of the means of production, and the contestation of that ownership.

57b. At the level of means of production, [premature] socialism bans any form of ownership, either private or social, together with the contestation of its specific absence. This means that premature socialism prohibits the most general forms in which interest can manifest itself.

58. The factual abolishment of private ownership of the means of production engenders a tendency toward the direct affirmation of needs which is rendered inoperative by scarcity and by the absence of social ownership.

59. The factual scarcity engenders a tendency toward the direct affirmation of interests which is rendered inoperative by the reality of a class structure which excludes the propertied classes.

59b. Reduced to the negation of interests, the affirmation of needs remains merely apparent. In a system of scarcity, needs can manifest themselves only as interests. This explains why the rejection of interests becomes the rejection of needs.

60. For its part, the market economy constantly generates and regenerates the mystification of needs as interests—interests that the social structure deprives of any ultimate purpose by preventing the formation of a class of private proprietors of the means of production.

61. A nonpolarized class structure should emancipate needs from their mystification as interests. Its opposition to the economic element is at the same an opposition toward interests.

62. The social order and the organization of the economy —the system of needs and the system of interests—thus prove incompatible. This explains why their unity cannot represent a system of synthesis but instead represents an antithesis reproduced independently by the command function.

63. The separation of needs from interests is manifested as a cleavage between the economy and the law. The law condemns the behaviors prompted by the economy. Thus the immediate effectiveness of the law is based not on its correspondence to actual relations but on the reality of the coercive means which impose it.

64. The restrictive force of the coercive means must be greater than the stimulus of the economic processes. Divorced from the economy, the law confines itself to legitimizing the unilateral exercise of coercion by the regime.

65. Freed from their mystification as interests, needs are in fact deprived of the only way available to them, under conditions of scarcity, of expressing themselves. Such liberation is tantamount to abandonment.

66. The producers, alienated from their product, are also alienated from their means of defense and organization. Through the stifling of interests, the organizations created to defend workers' interests lose their object, and hence their *raison d'etre*. Class struggles die out, and are replaced by the commands of the regime. The competitive system ends up as a system of centralized allocation.

67. To the capitalist mystification of needs as interests, centralized allocation opposes a double mystification: on the one hand it preserves the economic mechanisms that convert needs into interests, while on the other hand it prevents those mechanisms from acting in that direction.

68. The command system thus appears as the specific form

that premature socialism gives to the nonspecific contradiction between needs and interests.

69. The most general function of the arbitrary authority consists in reconciling an essentially capitalist process, industrialization, with the absence of capitalist-type proprietorship.

70. To achieve this, the regime exercises a dominant mediating function. This function places the regime above both the economic process and its false crystallization in the class structure—hence above society.

71. The class structure is created and imposed by the regime in spite of the market economy. And the market economy imposes itself on the regime by its spontaneous tendency to dissolve that structure.

72. As a result, the dominant mediation of the regime is expressed in a behavior differentiated with respect to each of the two elements. For a long period of time, its function is to reproduce their incompability and hence their coexistence. Confronted with a desirable social structure and an inevitable type of economy, the regime's behavior is also dichotomized: on the one hand, it systematically protects the class structure; on the other, it systematically disrupts the market economy.

72b. This disruptive function explains by itself the regime's tendency to take on a feudal-type organization, since it is this type of organization which has acquired the greatest wealth of historical experience as a disrupter of capitalist economic mechanisms.

73. Banned in both its private and social forms, property ceases to be the governing force in social life. This role reverts to the regime, which, by the very fact that it takes on such a role, loses its revolutionary character. For it opposes the personified law of the regime, something typical of the feudal system, to the impersonal laws of economic competition typical of capitalism.

74. To block impersonal competition under conditions of scarcity is to make the subjectivization of distribution economically necessary. The replacement of competition by a com-

mand system demands the replacement of impersonal allocation by personified allocation.

75. Thus it would seem that the command system puts an end to the capitalist dissolution of human relations into relations among objects.

76. In fact, however, this successful reconversion to personal relations is nothing more than a return to the relations of personal dependence that characterized precapitalism. The domination of man by scarcity thus assumes the reactionary form of personification.

77. The content of premature personification is not human relations but the old social relations of inequality.

78. The accidental nature of the market economy is subjected to the control of a political authority whose essence is precisely an accident as represented by the individual personifying the command system.

79. The essence of competition is choice. Therefore, the factual abolishment of competition implies the abolishment of alternatives. This way of organizing the absence of alternatives is concretized in the monolithism of the party, the supreme leader, the plan, the ideology, and public discourse; in the extreme univocity of the worker, and even in the ritualization of language.

80. The effective rejection of economic competition requires its replacement by a mechanism that represents not only noncompetitiveness but the very impossibility of competition [*l'incompétible*] : the arbitrary authority.

81. Economic competition is a way of distributing inequality. If all the competitors were equal before its laws, it would become dysfunctional. This is why total competition is something meaningless. Total knowledge and foresight would paralyze all competitive activity.

82. Thus the perfection of knowledge and foresight proves disastrous for competition. The command economy adopts for its own these conditions incompatible with competition.

83. The concept of perfection (and hence of infallibility)

assimilated by premature socialism is the convulsive expression of the rejection of competition. Incompatible with any modern social system, it is even more of an aberration for a socialist system. Its adoption represents the consummation of the reactionary organization of the regime. In projecting itself into mythology, the regime loses not only its revolutionary character but even its political complexion.

84. Recourse to infallibility is also a result of the excessive and premature rejection of the regulatory effect of the market. In this case, feedback is replaced by action, and hindsight is replaced by foresight. But the lack of feedback information has the result that foresight is transformed into prophecy.

85. Infallibility is thus a medieval solution for the contradiction, peculiar to premature socialism, between the rejection of information as expressed in the market, and the compulsion of foresight as expressed in the plan.

86. For that matter, a society can hardly accept the advantages of a command economy without tolerating, at the same time, the obligations inherent in it. To submit the arbitrary authority to a democratic audit by society would mean institutionalizing doubts concerning the legitimacy of that authority, and hence of its commands.

87. In order to be effective, the command authority has to be:

unique, hence extremely centralized;

stable, hence not subject to competition or to the whims of electoral systems;

infallible, hence charismatic and placed above the laws.

88. The social order can only be assured by the uniqueness of the arbitrary authority. Once the system is in place, this requirement takes on—within its limits—the force of a necessity. The official ideology expresses that necessity in the form of two fundamental principles:

monolithism, which justifies centralization;

the leading role of the party, which justifies charisma and the lack of competition.

89. A nonelective authority necessarily becomes a distributor of nonelectiveness. The construction of strong hierarchies based on relations of personal dependence presupposes the mandating of functions. Here, election is only the semblance of appointment. A true electoral system would be profoundly disturbing to the survival of the command system.

90. Therefore, to demand the democratization of premature socialism is tantamount to questioning the command economy and the system it has built for itself.

91. Political democracy is the complement of a competitive economy which is regulated impersonally and whose mechanisms are in principle accessible to all. Those impersonal laws —which under capitalism are frustrated by the domination of monopolies—are rejected by premature socialism, which opposes to them its command economy, whose complement is the immanent absence of political democracy.

92. Within the framework of a strategy of industrialization, the regime acts on the economy deliberately and effectively. But it is precisely the need to act in this way which becomes its principal shaper. By a nondeliberate process, the regime gradually acquires the traits that enable it to master the economy. Those traits confer upon its essentially anticapitalist orientation an essentially precapitalist complexion, since they are the traits of any arbitrary authority.

93. The conditioning of this regime, which believes itself to be unconditioned, lies essentially in this spontaneous adaptation to the combined pressures of underdevelopment and anticapitalist industrialization.

94. This conditioning is incorporated into the historical development of the regime. Its autonomy, which enabled the regime to avoid the danger of the dissolution of the new class structure in the process of industrialization, itself becomes, through that very achievement, the chief danger. For the more advanced the process of industrialization, the more unbearable the feudal organization of the regime directing it.

95. At the present level of industrialization, the feudal-

type opposition to the capitalist mechanisms of the economy represents a greater danger than those mechanisms themselves.

96. The unconditioned state of the regime is merely a shadow play of its unrecognized conditioning.

97. Unverified conditioning becomes nonselective adaptation to external impulses. The intrinsic structure of the regime is the sediment of extrinsic pressures to which it has adapted itself spontaneously.

98. The pragmatic regime opposes its own spontaneity to the spontaneity of the economy. The realm of necessity has changed its form, not its substance.

99. To study the present-day reality of premature socialism is to study the way in which it has let itself be shaped by its conditioning. To study its conditioning is, above all, to study the general laws of industrialization and those of coercion as expressed by the regime.

100. The task of anticapitalist industrialization is inescapable. What *is* avoidable is the spontaneous adaptation of the power structure to the retrogression of its allocative function.

101. The theoretically unchecked pressure of these objective factors endows the regime of premature socialism with traits that are markedly reactionary as compared to advanced capitalism.

102. Premature socialism has become divorced from the theoretical force that enabled its birth, and which it continues to evoke in its search for legitimacy. The abandonment of the theoretical approach implies submission to the constraints of the economy as expressed in industrialization, and of the regime as expressed in arbitrariness.

103. The remove between the initial theory and official ideology can be measured by the fact that the latter is nothing more than an apologia for the mutilations caused by the loss of the former.

104. No theory can do away with the inexorable impact of underdevelopment. But a Marxist theory of premature socialism would be capable of alleviating the damage caused by that im-

pact and, especially, of limiting its repercussions, in aggravating forms, on all aspects of social life—and primarily on the structure of the regime.

104b. The reactionary character of that regime is also made plain by the premodern complexion of the claims laid against it by the various movements aimed at improving it.

105. Premature socialism is a schizoid society: revolutionary by virtue of what it has snatched away from capitalism, reactionary by virtue of the power structure that it opposes to capitalism.

ABOUT THE AUTHOR

Felipe García Casals (a pseudonym) is a high-ranking official in an East European country.

Alfred G. Meyer, born in Germany and educated at Harvard University, is Professor of Political Science at the University of Michigan. He is the author of a number of books including *Marxism: the Unity of Theory and Practice*, *Leninism*, and *The Soviet Political System*.

Guy Daniels has published some fifty book translations from the Russian and French, chiefly in the fields of literature, history, and political science.